D1452415

DEINSTITUTIONALIZING
GOD

Cruddy,

Keep the faith!

DEINSTITUTIONALIZING
GOD

Much love,

Dionne Yvette Brown

A Minister's Journey on
Leaving Church to Save Her Faith

DIONNE YVETTE BROWN

Copyright © 2017, 2021 by Dionne Yvette Brown

All rights reserved. No part of this publication may be reproduced, distributed, or transmitted in any form or by any means, including photocopying, recording, or other electronic or mechanical methods, without the prior written permission of the author, except in the case of brief quotations embodied in critical reviews and certain other noncommercial uses permitted by copyright law.

To request permissions, contact info@dionnebrown.com

Cover Design: Manuella Lea Palmioli
Cover Picture: Jackie Hicks/Fond Memories Photography

ISBN 978-0-578-33180-5 (Hardcover)
ISBN 978-0-578-35710-2 (eBook)

Library of Congress Control Number: 2022900595

First Edition: 2022

Scripture marked NASB taken from the New American Standard Bible®, Copyright © 1960, 1971, 1977, 1995 by The Lockman Foundation. Used by permission.

Scripture marked NIV taken from the New International Version®, NIV® Copyright ©1973, 1978, 1984, 2011 by Biblica, Inc.®. Used by permission.

Scripture marked KJV taken from the Authorized King James Version.

Printed in the United States of America

To all who dared to believe,
but were disappointed

My Sabbath (236)

by Emily Dickinson

Some keep the Sabbath going to Church –
I keep it, staying at Home –
With a Bobolink for a Chorister –
And an Orchard, for a Dome –

Some keep the Sabbath in Surplice –
I, just wear my Wings –
And instead of tolling the Bell, for Church,
Our little Sexton – sings.

God preaches, a noted Clergyman –
And the sermon is never long,
So instead of getting to Heaven, at last –
I'm going, all along.

CONTENTS

PREFACE

This book was born out of my religious practice in the institutional church. It was either give expression to my reflections on faith or go insane. Literally. I was actually halfway there when I realized the church had beaten me to the crazy house. So here I am struggling with my conflicting experiences.

It is part spiritual memoir, part manifesto on the organized church, born of frustration with the inconsistencies between its witness and the reality of its impact. I wrote this book having just sent a formal letter withdrawing my membership from the congregation with which I had been affiliated for twelve years after being rejected for ordination. The separation was bittersweet as this was the place where my faith was restored after an acrimonious parting with my previous congregation and denomination.

Leaving church was not an option for me in the early stages of faith. I was raised to believe good, respectable people went to church every Sunday. Ironically, doing so did not bring out the best in me nor did it expose me to the highest inclinations of humanity. Church-hopping was generally frowned upon. You could visit other churches, but your name remained on the same roll and you passed that standing down to your children. I had planned to be funeralized at the same church I attended as a child. Is this the legacy Jesus left?

Stability was a virtue in my community of origin, for better and for worse. Divorce was not common, families seldom moved, and people retired from the same job after 30 to 40 soul-sucking years.

Writing this book was difficult. We do not talk about very personal issues in polite company and not much at all for that matter in my hometown of Washington, DC. There were so many conversations I was afraid of having with myself, let alone penning a narrative account for all who cared to read. I initially tried to conceal my story in abstract philosophical and theological ramblings so the limited audience could keep my confidence. The more I tried to write that way, the less I had to say.

This book was written for the victims of spiritual trauma who have been silenced, the prophetic voices that have been marginalized, and those with eyes to see who refuse to walk in darkness. Wherever you are, there are other deinstitutionalized believers who are willing to walk with you in faith. *God cannot be mocked!* All manner of religious foolishness will be called out for what it is and cast into the fire.

Maya Angelou said, "there is no greater agony than bearing an untold story inside you." Lots of people experiencing homelessness are on corners all over the world with masterpieces in their heads and great stories to tell. They are babbling, but no one is scribing their accounts. I was close to being one and wrote this book to release what was driving me crazy.

Staying out of a straightjacket has been my mission. It was either remain in the church, live a lie, and go crazy or be true to who I am in the kingdom and let the chips fall where they may. I could not complete this project until I fully integrated myself—intellectually, spiritually, and professionally. Now that I have, I can get on with the rest of my life and stop being defined by the experience of having been oppressed.

I am neither the first nor the last to recognize the contradictions in the church and try to find my place in spite of them. By the grace of God, I was enrolled in a seminar focused on one of the church's harshest critics—Danish theologian Søren Kierkegaard—as my own struggle reached crisis proportions. The Dane's writings saved my sanity. Hopefully mine will return the favor and help others to keep the faith.

The fact that I failed to attain something I restructured my entire life around was a source of shame. The reasons behind it were not my disgrace to bear. Then it came to me from every person I informed of this project that my story must be told and written plainly as the Lord instructed the prophet Habakkuk.

I tried to put the events behind me, but the memories lingered. They were impossible to purge despite my best efforts. Once I decided to unleash the secrets packed away so well in my inner life, a healing occurred that had been long elusive. Although wounds heal, the scars remain. Like Jesus Christ, I have taken the radical step of baring my scars to demonstrate the power of God.

Now in the throes of midlife, I had lived in more places, held more jobs, and belonged to more congregations than my parents have in their combined lifetimes. My only saving grace is that I do not have any failed marriages under my belt. That is not because I am so good at establishing and maintaining relationships. Au contraire! I have never been betrothed.

Leaving church is like the dissolution of a marriage. There is enough blame to go around and the parties are not as cordial as they pretend to be. I do not know whether I will ever join another congregation. The next leg of my journey is devoted to navigating my relationship with the divine without artificial constraints. I will leave the rest up to providence.

1

GENESIS OF THE MADNESS

Let us watch well our beginnings and the results will manage themselves.

Alexander Clark

Not everyone knows my name, but everyone knows my story. Searching for the Most High is a common human pursuit. People throughout history have staked a claim on having exclusive access to the divine and selling it on the marketplace of spiritual endeavor. Packaging God is an exercise in futility. I learned that the hard way by overinvesting in organized religion and being let down each and every time. The places where I and like-minded individuals have a reasonable expectation that we would find love is often the last place we encounter it.

God called me to preach the gospel. I did not ask for the assignment or assume the role of my own volition. How my life would have been better in a lot of ways had God just left me alone crossed my mind with great frequency. The institutional church has blocked access to the profession consistently during my pursuit of ministry. I expected opposition from The Adversary, but not from the people calling themselves the Body of Christ.

I am not anyone of note. The church reminds me of such constantly, but God loves me lavishly. I have endured all manner of insanity trying to work out my soul's salvation. Absurdities and injuries that would be dealbreakers in any other context often get negotiated away by the higher purpose of communities of faith. However, indulging such is not my ministry. What passes for godliness is an affront to those of us who recognize Christendom for what it really is. I, personally, can no longer go on pretending. The real and psychological costs are too high.

I do not know who I was before being institutionalized spiritually. I was only around five years-old when I began attending church. The Lord who came to draw a sword between my parents and me did not secure the union between me and the households of faith I joined. The ties formed at my previous churches were not as binding as I assumed. Congregations basically tell you not to let the door hit you when you decide to leave. All efforts to remain in fellowship have been at my initiative. Yet, my natural parents have always awaited their prodigal daughter with open arms.

It has been said that every tragic hero has an endangered infancy narrative. Zeus, Moses, Jesus, Superman, and so it is with me. My story began when Hilda Brown felt a familiar sensation having given birth to three children before. She took a taxi to DC General Hospital while her husband, Tommy, remained behind at home with their other children and an NFL game in-progress on television. It was his reasonable sacrifice. By the time Hilda arrived at the hospital, she was in the latter stages of labor and the baby was descending down the birth canal.

Mom burst into tears earlier in the year when her doctor announced she was pregnant again. The stress of raising four small children—including one stepchild—was wearing on her. The physician offered to induce labor early and allow the fetus to suffocate due to underdeveloped lungs. Mom collected her bearings after visualizing such an act and yelled "you will not kill my baby!" She read to her growing belly and listened to lots of music by Dionne Warwick, hence the name.

On Sunday, September 22, 1968, the emergency room staff rushed her to the delivery room where I entered the world anticlimactically. The attending physician slapped my bottom to prompt my first cry. According to my mother, I looked wide-eyed at him and did not make a sound. He hit me a second time with the same result. Upon the third time, I cleared my little baby throat as if to issue a warning.

From that point on, I continued to defy expected norms. The trip to the nursery was my first act of rebellion. I cried while the other babies slept and slept while they cried. The nurses' attempts to put me on a schedule failed. Therefore, I was expelled from the nursery at DC General Hospital for the remainder of our stay and committed to my mother's room. I have been put out of much finer establishments since then.

You might be wondering why I know this story so well. Every year on September 22nd, my mother calls me at the exact time of my birth to recount this series of events. No matter where I am or what I am doing, I must make myself available at 8:24pm for this annual ritual. It is like our own personal Pesach Haggadah. She does not have a dramatic birth narrative for any of her other children. Guess they must not be tragic heroes.

My childhood was pretty uneventful. My siblings and I shared what passed for normal growing up in the Nation's Capital at the time. Then one Sunday afternoon my maternal great aunt, Gertrude, stopped by our house for a visit. Her uniform included cat glasses, a conservative dress, a very sturdy purse, and sensible shoes regardless of what day of the week it was. Aunt Gert expressed shock and horror to my parents that their children did not attend church.

She must have counted them as damned because she did not even inquire about their religious habits. But Aunt Gert told my parents that under no uncertain terms should we be allowed to stay home on Sunday mornings watching The Little Rascals, Tarzan, and Elvis movies on television. Members of my family either attended church forcibly as children or became holy rollers after becoming exhausted from raising all the hell they could muster. There was nothing in-between.

So, in kindergarten, I began attending Sunday School at an African Methodist Episcopal (AME) church about six blocks away. A strange twist of fate sent us there as several churches of other denominational affiliation were closer to home. My sister Crystal and her best friend, Dee Dee, were members and belonged to its Camp Fire Girls program.

My siblings and I attended Ward Memorial AME Church fifty-two Sundays a year with no exceptions. It was not that my parents were so convicted by Aunt Gert's meddling, but rather blown away that they had not discovered this source of free babysitting sooner. We grew to hate Aunt

Gert more and more with each passing year. The novelty of a new weekly outing grew into contempt for such a major disruption in our lives.

A foot of snow fell overnight one Saturday, but the Brown children were at the locked doors of the church Sunday morning right on cue. Other parents caught on to this childcare hustle one by one and it soon became a neighborhood affair. So many of us paraded together through the streets weekly that we probably needed a permit.

The church is named after Thomas M. D. Ward, the 10th Bishop of the AME Church. The congregation first formed in 1877 and was known then as Grace Chapel AME Church. The original edifice was a modest wood frame structure. The current brick sanctuary was built on the corner of 42nd and Brooks Streets NE in 1955. The addition of a large multipurpose room came later in the early 1980s. Its choirs are legendary. Its members have also been known through the years to be very involved in the connectional church.

It is said that Black people do not join country clubs; they go to church. Although Ward was in a predominantly working- and lower middle-class neighborhood, it was associated with a broader bourgeois organization. My siblings and friends were not quite as welcome because we were not their kind of people. We were well-groomed and dressed appropriately, but church members could not associate us with our families of origin. It also did not help that we were also free of decorum and theological commitments.

Today, we have a multitude of ways of signaling our social position. When people ask for your church affiliation, it is seldom a theological inquiry. They are usually trying to peep your pedigree or social station. Therefore, these bodies are struggling with their relevance in the modern era—less in an existential sense than to pay their bills. On the other hand, many other congregations have fled the city and transplanted into affluent suburbs more suitable to their aspirations. As I walk the streets of Washington, DC, I notice no shortage of large, stately edifices that once housed thriving congregations. You can have a whole pew to yourself on most Sundays.

James Baldwin said, "The people who call themselves 'born again' today have simply become members of the richest, most exclusive private club in the world, a club that the man from Galilee could not possibly hope—or wish—to enter."[1] Well, this particular sect was a carefully curated group striving to social climb as members of one of the most esteemed denominations in Black America. We were not elevating their status, discipleship notwithstanding.

As the weeks turned to months and the months turned to years, my crowd realized we did not fit in. The children who were not of our set behaved differently. They entered orderly, sang hymns robotically, and sat unnervingly blank as the teachers read recycled lessons from little booklets with pictures of white people they said were from places where the native inhabitants were of color.

They were like little Stepford children whose parents were less concerned about their soul salvation than social control. "Teach them to be well-behaved, drug-free, and sexually abstinent however you can" were their orders. "If they get too deep into Jesus our cover might be blown." We did not have that kind of pressure on us. Our parents were simply content to have the house to themselves for a few hours a week.

Much to our Sunday School teachers' chagrin, we brought the fun. The lessons began with biblical passages followed by stale narratives that did not connect with our reality and what we should glean from them. Free from our parents' oversight and the desire to be accepted, we could get loose. It did not help that the day before, we likely saw an age-inappropriate film at the neighborhood movie theater. Almost every Saturday, we likewise walked to The Senator where we watched Blaxploitation, horror, and Kung Fu films without adult supervision.

We were the first generation of the post-Civil Rights era growing up in Chocolate City, no less. Social justice, not social climbing was the aspect of the gospel that captured us. "Prepare us for the revolution!" we begged. Little did we know, we were not supposed to engage them. We were supposed to swallow the lessons from the pre-printed guides whole. "Forget about loving God with all your heart, soul, and mind" the teachers insinuated. "Drink the Kool-Aid."

Well, being from the 'hood breeds a healthy sense of skepticism. "I hear you talking, but is what you're telling us really in the Bible?" "Is that what God is really saying there?" "Do you adhere to these teachings yourself or are they just for us?" "What's the deal with eating flesh and drinking blood?" They were not ready.

This was before the era of megachurches and large multipurpose buildings. Each class occupied a small section in the medium-sized sanctuary separated only by a few rows of pews. At any given time, one of the faithful teachers could be heard breathing a sigh of exasperation at the children who would not fall into formation. Within an hour or so, the weekly ritual came to an end and we would depart with glee recounting the good time we just had.

Some of the children whose parents also attended Ward Memorial lived in the neighborhood and thus went to school with us. Therefore, the relationships transcended Sunday mornings. I learned how they were invited to social activities at other church members' homes and connectional church events. The presence of my crew's company was not requested as much. It was all good though. We lived in a tight-knit community and had each other.

Deanwood, the neighborhood from which I hail, is in the far-Northeast section of the city, east of the Anacostia River. It is one of the few areas of DC that has always been predominantly Black. The early community was almost rural in nature. New housing was built after World-War II to accommodate Black veterans buying houses with government benefits and Blacks displaced by urban renewal in western parts of the city. Being born the year Martin Luther King died, the aftermath of the riots served as a backdrop to my childhood. Many areas of the city looked just the same thirty to forty years later.

My Sunday School education was complemented by a radical shift in public education and Black Nationalist politics. The junior high school I attended was named after the esteemed educator Kelly Miller. My high school's colors were red, black, and green with an African warrior holding a spear in one hand and a shield in the other as its mascot. That was all perfectly normal for the time and place. Our teachers were preparing the Black Power generation to take our rightful place in the world. We studied things that were not in the authorized curriculum. We had activists in the movement as guest speakers. Our consciousness was raised and our voices tuned to stake our claim on the promise of the

American Dream. Excessive standardized testing and so-called school reform are ensuring that never happens again.

The Watergate scandal broke within my first year of attending Sunday School and with it my political birth. I remember waiting for my father to get home from work on August 8, 1974. He was a laborer at the U.S. Capitol and would surely be abreast of what this event meant for the nation. It was all over the news and networks suspended their regularly scheduled programming. I knew he was not a member of Congress or one of their professional staffers, but expected him to fill me in nonetheless. I am a fourth generation Washingtonian on his side of the family, hence the natural proclivity for politics. Never did Daddy talk down to me or shun my questions. This became an ongoing part of our routine, in addition to watching the news show *60 Minutes* every Sunday evening following the week's football games.

When I was in the eighth grade, I told my social studies teacher I aspired to earn a PhD. She subsequently sat with me after school and walked me through her Master's thesis. That same year, I told the Superintendent of Sunday School I wanted to be baptized. I cannot say my request was grounded in a particular religious experience, but it seemed like the logical thing to do as I matured into adolescence. Almost all of the children of established families in the church had been baptized as babies or small children, although with little to no recollection. The church had led me to profess Jesus Christ as Lord and taught me about the importance of the sacrament, but said it was not available to me because my parents were not members. I felt so dejected. Why wouldn't they let me in?

Our Lord and Savior was not baptized until adulthood. On the other hand, Jesus said, *let the little children come to me, and do not hinder them, for the kingdom of heaven belongs to such as these.* Not easily deterred, I asked again the following year and every year thereafter to no avail.

Babies were baptized on the day of their birth in colonial America to swell the rolls of the church. Thomas Jefferson refused to endorse attempts to require infant baptism under law. As one of the drafters of the U.S. Constitution, he was the brainpower behind the First Amendment clause forbidding the establishment of religion by the government. Leaving the exercise of faith to personal choice was a gift to believers and nonbelievers alike. If God did not want humanity to exercise choice, we would not have been endowed with free will.

It is no secret that mainline Protestant churches are in decline. Have those who inflate their rolls by forcing membership upon those born into their constituent families considered that might be part of the problem? Socialization into faith is no substitute for true discipleship. Protestant theologians argued during the Reformation that one cannot impute their faith to another. Yet, the church persists in perpetuating this falsehood.

One of my best childhood friends would not leave her eternal destiny to chance. Being strong-willed by nature, Neptina opted to get baptized that summer at Morning Star, the neighborhood Pentecostal church where we attended Vacation Bible School. They baptized anyone confessing Jesus as Lord. Express the desire and you got dunked with a quickness. With her salvation secured, Neptina elevated her participation at Ward Memorial by remaining for eleven o'clock service after Sunday School. A few neighborhood friends and I accompanied her because we had nothing else to do.

My pastor, Rev. James H. Robinson, used to implore parishioners to question him regarding his sermons and provide feedback. My neighborhood friends and I would discuss the day's message during our walk home, but never found any occasion to raise an issue. I would go a step further and review the relevant passages of Scripture at home in the study Bible gifted to me by the Sunday School. Never did I feel the need to challenge anything he said.

My parents gave us the option of no longer attending church upon graduating high school or turning eighteen—whichever came first. Each of my siblings took them up on that offer as they reached their respective milestones. My neighborhood friends did the same. I had no intention on continuing with church attendance as an adult either. The members made it abundantly clear, or so I thought, that I was an outsider crashing their party. The congregation offered generous college scholarships, but I did not apply during my senior year because I was through with them.

Then came the day that will forever live in infamy. Early on the morning of June 19, 1986, University of Maryland basketball star Len Bias died of a cocaine-induced heart attack. It rocked my world not only because I watched him play on television religiously, but also because I happened to be on campus the night he died. Some friends and I were riding around aimlessly because we were too young to get in the club. I was excited to be an incoming freshman and took every opportunity to visit Maryland's campus. The news report from the digital clock radio on the nightstand next to my bed shook me to my core as I awakened. I cried for days like he was my best friend. My decision to attend the University of Maryland was based solely on being a devoted fan of their football and basketball teams. I attended a summer college preparatory program there while in high school during which I got to meet many of my heroes, including Len Bias.

This was unbelievable as he had just been selected in the first round of the NBA draft by the Boston Celtics. His star came crashing down as soon as it reached its peak. This was my first existential crisis. I began to question whether anything was worth striving for if death was our ultimate end. Within a few weeks, I resumed my summer fun in anticipation of college life. Len Bias' death certainly imposed a new limit on how far I would go in my debauchery. I drank, but never did drugs. They were all around and some friends were frequent users. He probably saved my life, as well as countless others.

Ironically, church attendance was the furthest thing from my mind when I moved eight long miles away to College Park to attend the University of Maryland. I adhered to faith in an abstract sense, but nothing in my behavior or habits indicated such in the secular environment of the state's sprawling flagship campus. Playboy magazine ranked Maryland annually as one of the nation's top party schools in the 1980s and it earned that designation. During my first weekend on campus, a DJ out of Baltimore named Frank Ski rocked so hard that everyone left Preinkert Gymnasium drenched with sweat. We partied with abandon in College Park. If we were not jamming in one of the large ballrooms in the Student Union or a local nightclub, we were crowded in a campus dorm room or leaning on a bar somewhere. Interspersed with all that revelry were activities suited to every interest, lascivious affairs, and the obligatory classes.

I came home for the summer at the end of my freshman year on top of the world. It was not due to newfound hope that I was headed for a brighter future. It was because I had just had the best year of my life. However, being a creature of habit got the best of me. The first Sunday of my summer vacation, I returned to Ward Memorial and every week thereafter. My perennial request to be baptized was met with an indifferent response. "Well, you're an adult now. We can't stop you."

On June 21, 1987, I marched down the aisle enthusiastically when candidates for baptism were called during the worship service. Nobody usually responded to the invitation on third Sundays and the liturgy would advance to the next part of the service. It took me a while to get to the altar as I always sat in the rear pews feeling like an imposter. The congregation seemed surprised, but unmoved, that they had a live one. They listened attentively as the ceremony began and smiled affirmatively.

My decision was more an aesthetic and ethical choice than a religious one. My new dress was reminiscent of the old-world glamour of Audrey Hepburn. It was a white sheath with a matching elbow sleeve bolero jacket. Matching shoes and purse were de rigueur. I passed on gloves. This was an important occasion before some very important people so I had to look the part. Most adults in the congregation had moved to DC from the South during the Great Migration in search of better economic prospects. Ward came highly recommended as a very traditional and politically influential congregation. The men always dressed impeccably regardless of what they did for a living and were perfect gentlemen. I had been studying the church ladies for years. These were fancy women who dressed with a classic sense of taste, were well-coiffed, and carried themselves with grace.

None of my family members or friends outside of the church were present for my baptism. I told them about it, but did not issue formal invitations. Being that the third Sunday in June was also Father's Day, the congregation was also celebrating Men's Day. Therefore, Frederick Calhoun James, the 93rd Bishop of the AME Church, served as the guest speaker. I was rather disappointed not to be baptized by the man who had been my pastor for most of my life at that point. I thought to myself, "Who is this joker?" Never did the honor of being baptized by an ecclesiastical leader dawn on me at the time.

I had no expectations when I stood at the altar as the sole candidate for the day. Rev. Robinson read an oath from the hymnal about renouncing the devil, keeping God's commandments, and walking henceforth in faith. Nothing he said left a lasting impression. I was just checking a box thinking that singular act got my name into the Lamb's Book of Life. Then Rev. Robinson turned the ritual over to Bishop James, who incidentally, was wearing a much fancier robe than him.

The stewardesses removed the cover from the wooden baptismal font on the altar to reveal a water-filled vessel and lovingly wrapped a white towel around my neck. The prelate said something about the significance of what I was doing. Bishop James then placed his hand in the water three times in a measured cadence saying "I baptize you in the name of the Father, of the Son, and of the Holy Ghost." Something came over me as he palmed my forehead with his hand to sprinkle me the third time and I wept uncontrollably. The stewardesses embraced me and wiped my tears until I regained a sense of composure while the organist played softly. Like the remainder of my faith journey, I walked to my seat alone into the unknown.

I returned to the University of Maryland for my sophomore year unchanged. New members' classes were in order during my return the following summer. A lay member of the congregation led us through the history, doctrine, and discipline of the AME Church. Those of us who completed that series were called in front of the congregation to be received into full membership following a litany in the AME Church Hymnal.

Rev. Robinson asked a series of questions about our faith and commitment to the denomination. He ordered us to face the congregation and asked whether there was any reason we should not be received. No one ever objected to new members. Then Rev. Robinson extended us the right hand of fellowship. The officers subsequently approached us with outstretched hands, followed by members singing "What a fellowship, what a joy divine." Nothing about the process made me feel like my standing before God had changed. I was now just a card-carrying member of the AME Church.

My church attendance during holidays and breaks from college was less a matter of faith than like salmon returning home to spawn. That is actually literal because at this point, I had a boyfriend who was a member of one of the most respected families at church. In his mind and many others, I was dating up despite his cocaine addiction. He eventually died of a drug overdose.

I became more acceptable to church members as I pursued higher education and embarked on a professional career. They did not inquire about my faith development over the years, but were more interested in the improvement in my social and economic status. Members have even commended me for "making something of yourself." Meanwhile, many of their children have not fulfilled their hopes for upward mobility.

The first thing I recall praying for fervently was not at all religious. It was membership in a sorority. Greekdom was the center of life among the 44,000 students at the University of Maryland. Large fraternity and sorority houses greet one on the drive down Route One past the main entrances to the campus. Although they did not have campus houses, Greekdom was even more central for the 4,000 or so Black students. Predominantly white sororities and fraternities held rushes during the fall semester, allowing freshmen to pledge soon after arrival. Black Greek-lettered organizations typically required at least one year of academic attainment for membership eligibility.

During the spring of my freshman year, I was caught off guard by young women and men suddenly marching around campus in-line and dressed alike. I knew about sororities and fraternities, but had not seen them in action beyond a party. Walking in unison was a form of group synchrony to instill the discipline of working together cooperatively. Dressing alike removed any distinctions between members. The pledges drew a lot of admiration and attention as each of the eight chapters of Black Greek-lettered organizations on campus had a line that semester. I wanted in on that.

Acceptance in a sorority or fraternity was pretty challenging on such a large campus. Many prospectives vied for each available slot. Making your intentions known put one in a vulnerable position with the members whose approval was necessary. Some of the criteria were straightforward such as a certain grade point average, good moral character, and a record of community service. Others were shallow, petty, and superfluous. Being a legacy helped one's chances. Neither my mother nor my three sisters were members so I could not count on that. My sophomore year was too out of control to present myself for scrutiny. I was deliberately more reserved and focused junior year. Nothing mattered more at that time.

Everything I earned until this point came relatively easy. The competitive pursuit of membership in the sorority of my choice required some extra help. My grades were decent. They had to be or my dad would have kept me home and forced me to attend the University of the District of Columbia as he threatened when he opened my grades at the end of each semester. I was a known quantity on campus and an officer in the campus chapter of the NAACP. However, there were many other young ladies equally qualified. So, I prayed. All. The. Time. I prayed first thing in the morning. I chanted while walking across campus to class. I prayed before bedtime. And I got in.

One Sunday morning about a year later, I awakened in my campus apartment to greet the beginning of the week by preparing a large breakfast as is the custom in my family. What I fixed that particular day, I cannot remember. It could have been a tall stack of pancakes or something equally filling. It had to be something with staying power because it had to last while I basked in reading *The Washington Post* from cover to cover.

Afterward, I stole away into my bedroom to listen to the broadcast of the worship service on WHUR, Howard University's radio station. Rankin Chapel has been described as the national cathedral of Black America. The best and most prophetic voices are invited to deliver a word that reaches far beyond the Mecca of Black academia.

If you are among the stellar, you get invited back year after year. Think Samuel Proctor, Benjamin E. Mays, Gardener C. Taylor, Floyd Flake, Jeremiah Wright, and Wyatt Tee Walker. Even non-clergy such as Frederick Douglass, Mary McLeod Bethune, and W. E. B. DuBois have prophesied there. Of course, Martin Luther King, Jr. graced its pulpit. Even non-Black leaders such as John F. Kennedy, Eleanor Roosevelt, and theologian Reinhold Niebuhr have spoken there. It is truly a special place.

This particular morning, I was excited to hear a message from Vashti Murphy McKenzie not only because she was one of the leading voices among Black female preachers, but also because I was a neophyte of Delta Sigma Theta Sorority, Inc. She was not only a member, but also the granddaughter of one of our Founders and our National Chaplain.

When that fire is newly lit, one takes every opportunity to immerse oneself into different aspects of one's organization. It is very likely that just the evening before, I attended a party surrounded by my linesisters and prophytes as we did every weekend.

I was not particularly religious in college. As a matter of fact, I was anything but. Those years represented the opportunity to raise all kinds of hell like in the coming-of-age movies I watched growing up. I was a consummate nerd in high school. My parents never had to make me do my homework. I visited the library for fun and never partied or dated. That all changed when I got to Maryland. Going away to college was also a relief from the requirement to attend church every Sunday. We had a large chapel on campus that I never visited for anything, save for special events that happened to be hosted there.

But God has a way of keeping me reined in. Little did I know before pursuing membership that my Sorority was founded on Christian principles. The readings during our ritualistic activities watered the seeds planted deeply within. That, coupled with the Rankin Chapel broadcasts, reignited my faith. I listened to them on my boom box at a much lower volume than I would blast my Go-Go, house, R&B, or rap music. It was my secret affair on Sunday mornings. I would close the door to my cramped bedroom, tune in, and listen attentively as if I were creeping with an illicit lover.

So there I was listening to the choir sing songs of Zion in anticipation of my revered Soror's delivery. Her form was quite familiar as a minister within the AME tradition. I cannot recall specifically anything she said, but do recall getting happy. Being from a more staid congregation, that was not a frequent occurrence. The choir back home sang stirring anthems and traditional hymns. Handclapping during the occasional upbeat song and scattered "amens" during the sermon were about as raucous as our worship got.

Then something within me started vibing with her proclamation of the Word in a way I had never experienced before. I found myself following her flow with connectivity almost to the point where I felt like I could pick up where she left off. This was the first time I felt the urge to preach. I did not know it real-time or at least not consciously. Later that week, I was meeting with the President of the Black Student

Union as the President of the College Park Chapter of the NAACP. The hot-button political topic we were discussing made me announce that I wanted want to preach about it. Couldn't be. Had to be a figure of speech. I packed that proclivity away in a panic as best I could.

At the time, I had no sense that a call to ministry was an actual phenomenon. In my eyes, ministers chose the profession voluntarily. None I had encountered at that young age seemed to be struggling with whether or not to be a part of the profession. We had a youth minister at Ward Memorial who seemed very happy about his vocation, our behavior notwithstanding. My pastor was an educated professional who I thought was too talented for the position. I could not make sense of why the gravitational pull toward the gospel ministry came to me all of a sudden. But my high aspirations for a political and academic career were hellbent on suppressing it.

The following summer, I returned home to continue partying without the inconvenience of classes. However, when the Superintendent of Sunday School solicited for Vacation Bible School teachers, I was among the first to respond. I returned to school that fall and fell back into my routine of studying, partying, and carousing, in no particular order. It was as if the previous religious experiences never happened. Then the following summer, I did it again—attending church every Sunday and participating in Vacation Bible School actively. Not only did I teach that year, but I marched my nieces and some neighborhood children to church every evening.

The difference that year was my collegiate career had ended and thus did my non-stop partying. During my exit interview, the director of my undergraduate program encouraged me warmly. He said he saw the mark of greatness on me (the first person other than my mother to say so) and further inquired what I planned to do with my life. I replied with all sincerity, "I don't know; but when you see me on Oprah, I have fulfilled my purpose."

Receiving my degree during the George H.W. Bush recession, I had no choice except to pursue graduate studies. The administrative job I had in the federal government did not appeal to me as a career. My white supervisor told me I was only qualified to be a secretary although my white peers were automatically promoted into professional, career ladder positions prior to graduating. She was very senior in the organization despite not having a degree herself. My father grumbled at graduation that he wanted his money back, stating that I was smarter before I went to college.

The next year was filled with studying for the GRE, researching public service-related graduate programs, and working my brain-numbing job to save money for school. It was also chock full of happy hours, clubbing, and parties. My decision-making process had all of the rationality cultivated during my undergraduate years. Ohio State University awarded me a full fellowship with a substantial stipend to attend graduate school there at the home of my new favorite Division I football team after the collapse of Maryland's athletics following the Len Bias scandal.

However, my visit to Duke University reeled me in in every way. The fact that it was esteemed highly academically was incidental. Duke was my favorite NCAA Division I men's basketball team and my Hail Mary choice. They had just won a second consecutive National Championship the week of my arrival. Spirits were flying high all over campus and t-shirts were hot off the presses in the bookstore. The campus was also scenic and meticulously groomed. They cut the grass and trimmed the hedges every day at Duke. Literally. Maryland's state-funded budget did not provide for such opulence.

My parents rejoiced at being off the hook financially, assuming I had accepted Ohio State's generous offer. It was only when they overheard me on the telephone searching for an apartment in North Carolina did they sense my pipe dream of attending Duke was becoming a reality.

"What in the world are you doing?" they asked with a shocked incredulity.

"They let me in so I'm going," I replied.

They shook their heads at me dismissively as they had so many times before.

My father got over his disappointment when he submitted his leave slip to move me to Durham, North Carolina in August of 1992. Nobody batted an eye when he packed his station wagon to take me and all my belongings to College Park. But everybody wanted to know how he, of all people, was able to send his daughter to such a prestigious university. My father never went past high school and worked as a sheet metal mechanic for the Architect of the Capitol, the agency responsible for the maintenance, operation, development, and preservation of the buildings and land throughout Capitol Hill.

To his Black peers, Daddy became a bigshot for setting his baby girl up so nicely. To his white co-workers, he became an object of contempt. He took it in stride and wore his "Duke Dad" shirt with pride. I was always proud that my father worked at the Capitol and looked him up whenever I was in the building on a field trip—from elementary through graduate school.

Walking the sacred ground across Duke Chapel's lawn every day seemed to have caused me to absorb faith by osmosis while pursuing a Master of Public Policy. It is a tall, majestic building that takes your breath away. Driving through the canopy of trees along the main entrance to campus during my prospective student visit was akin to approaching Cinderella's Castle rising to meet the horizon. Hence, some refer to the university as "Gothic Disneyland."

This was my first time away from home having gone to college inside Washington's beltway. Approaching the North Carolina state line put me in a different state of being as my moving van cruised down I-85 and still does to this day. I attended Sunday services at the Chapel immediately upon matriculation at Duke. The Divinity School's library also became the setting for my studies with seminarians I met on the shuttle bus. Little did I know what was occurring.

High church was quite familiar to me having been raised in an AME congregation that was heavy on the "E". The Dean of the Chapel at the time was the very prolific preacher, William Willimon. I had never heard of him before and only attended services there because the chapel was walking distance from my off-campus apartment. It felt like everything he said resonated with me deeply. Although I had not planned consciously to be a regular, I became one during my first semester.

However, Black students deplored my decision and encouraged me to attend a more culturally-appropriate church instead. The racial climate on campus proved to be hostile to say the least. Although I had a history of depression, being at Duke was the first time I reached the point of having to pursue clinical intervention. Finding the closest AME church provided not only a respite from constant insults and microaggressions, it also gave me a sense of familiarity.

Attending Duke was a great culture shock. The first reason was that almost everyone was rich. The University of Maryland was a solidly middle-class school with not much variance in either direction. Maryland was also different in the respect that most students were raised in racially and economically diverse communities. Duke students consistently rate as the wealthiest across the nation and come from very insular environments. I could not even pretend to be on their level financially. Connecting with them socially was wholly another question.

I was the only Black student in my class of twenty-seven. I was also the only one in the entire program my second year as no Blacks matriculated in the following class. This was a first for me. The sense of alienation was compounded by the collaborative nature of my program requiring each cohort to spend almost all its waking hours together. The wealthiest students were generally the coolest as nobody or nothing posed a threat to them. It astounded some of my classmates that I came from a two-parent household, had never been on welfare, and spoke so well. The sight of deliverymen in the lobby excited me just to see another Black face in passing.

Suffice to say, some professors and classmates alike thought I had stolen some more deserving white person's right to be there simply because of the color of my skin. They often went to great lengths to make their positions clear. The unfiltered classroom conversations revealed the roots of racial tensions in America in a manner to which I had not been exposed previously. Whenever matters of race arose, they looked to me to address them on behalf of Black people everywhere and charged it to incompetence when I refused.

The professors were as unenlightened as the students. Issues with racial undertones were addressed anecdotally as opposed to the scholarship afforded to other topics. There also was not a single Black professor on the program's faculty at the time. A Black college student at a predominantly white institution captured my sentiments perfectly a generation before me. "I came here to be a student, not to educate whites about Blacks. I'm tired of being an unpaid, untenured professor teaching these guys the elements of humanity."[2] The stress began to take its toll. I needed an outlet.

The services at St. Joseph AME followed the same traditional order of worship as my home church in DC, but the messages were more convicting of the need to attain more in faith. Church overall was different in the South. People acted like they were Jesus' first cousins and knew God's middle name. It was there that I first heard a fire and brimstone sermon. The message got my attention and made me aware that I was hell-bound if I did not make some changes.

By the grace of God, I got out of Duke with my sanity intact and a diploma with all the rights and privileges appertaining thereunto. Like Richard Pryor's character Mudbone, "I wasn't mad no more either." A Duke alum recruited me as a health policy analyst at the management consulting firm where he served as Executive Vice President. The work was exciting as health reform was a leading issue following the failure of the plan proposed by Hillary Clinton. Some exciting projects presented themselves as both the public and private sectors sought to mitigate the need for legislative intervention for improving the industry. I worked strenuous hours and took advantage of every opportunity to expand my boundaries. One of my senior managers said part of the reason they hired me was because the company recognized the level of resilience required for me to get through Duke as a Black woman would serve me well there.

Although work was fulfilling, there was something more for which I longed. Once I got established in my position, I left the congregation of my youth to join another congregation of the same denomination in the city—Allen Chapel AME Church. That was not such a huge departure since I maintained social ties to Ward Memorial and encountered its members at connectional church events. Fervent Bible study, constant activities, and charismatic worship seemed like a more authentic expression of faith. About a year later, I discerned my call to the gospel ministry and jumped into the pool headfirst. Was it the Lord or the Prozac talking? Only time would tell.

2

VOLUNTARY COMMITMENT

God loved the birds and invented trees. Man loved the birds and invented cages.

Jacques Deval

At Ward Memorial, I was a basically a Sunday worshipper and usher, with an occasional activity here and there. Although I had good religious form, my spirit remained underdeveloped. The canon as a cohesive unit was foreign to me and I could not leverage the power at work in me. Such did not suit my sensibilities as an information junkie and classic overachiever. Attending multiple services on Sunday, several Bible studies each week, annual retreats, and denominational activities became my routine at Allen Chapel. Not only that, friends and I visited one another's churches in the same manner we party-hopped.

Make no mistake; my inner party girl was still alive and kicking. No matter how late I stayed out Saturday night, I still managed to make it to worship Sunday morning. If I stayed out until daybreak, I did not even bother going to sleep. This was the first time I took the leap from being an arbitrary donor to tithing. Ward, in its modesty, did not pressure members on how much to give. Their sanctuary was built in 1955. The mortgage had been long since burned. Allen Chapel, on the other hand, had a new sanctuary and thus had bills to pay. Tithing was not much of a personal sacrifice as it just cut into my disposable income. I was all-in with this crowd, but later learned too much of a good thing is more than a notion.

Allen Chapel's congregation was larger and more economically diverse, but not as well-heeled and politically connected as Ward's. They had a large sanctuary located deeper in the 'hood, with an attached multipurpose building and off-street parking. Their original building was the same size as Ward Memorial, but they expanded about five years before I joined. Allen is located in the Garfield Heights neighborhood of Southeast Washington, surrounded by apartments and low-income housing. The distinctions between who lived where and who had what were not as stark as at Ward. People from the nearby neighborhood were just as active and influential at Allen Chapel as those who commuted from large suburban homes. The culture made it a place where I could let my hair down and worship more uninhibitedly.

From the moment I joined Allen, the pastor (henceforth referred to as "Rev.") and I seemed to have a warm pastoral relationship. I never felt the need to be guarded early on as he never behaved inappropriately and was old enough to be my grandfather. We chewed the fat quite frequently and were mutually complimentary of each other's sartorial proficiency. I know how to pull a look together because my father and grandfather worked in the corridors of Capitol Hill, although in a blue-collar capacity. They taught me the value of quality over quantity and the virtue of restraint. From the time I started my first professional position, I was looking and playing the part above my paygrade. Like my father and grandfather, Rev. made a career in the federal government and had surely studied how those in power carry themselves. Unlike the men in my family, he lacked social polish due to the lack of formality in his work environment at the General Printing Office or proximity to its leaders.

We exchanged pleasantries in church, but did not interact much beyond that. One evening only a few months after I joined Allen Chapel, Rev. invited my high school classmate who introduced me to the church and me to accompany him to an event across town where he was being presented with an award for community service. We met at the church after work and I chauffeured him to the banquet at a downtown hotel. A male minister of his acquaintance, about a decade older than me, joined us at a restaurant for dinner afterward.

We all exchanged business cards with him at the end of the evening. I did not think anything of it. The minister began calling me on the telephone. None of the conversations were of religious import. Turns out he had separated from his wife and was trying to line up sexual options. When I informed him that I do not practice adultery, he tried in vain to convince me it was acceptable. Even if he had not been married, his shallowness, mediocre looks, and cheap suit did not appeal to me. Little did I know how that evening portended how the dynamics between Rev. and me would take shape.

When the call came, I did not ask many questions. Honestly, I thought I was crazy when I discerned my call to preach. Friends, church members, and complete strangers had told me a zillion times that I should be preaching. However, being a member of the clergy did not conform with my self-image. Preachers do not get invited to the best parties. People always censor themselves in their company. And the most ethical ones have too much integrity to maximize their potential. So, I went about building a life that did not satisfy or seem to be going anywhere despite outward appearances of success.

Allen Chapel held fall revival the week before Thanksgiving 1995 and, of course, I attended every night. The guest preacher was Rev. David Durham, a legendary Washington-based pastor with phenomenal recall of Scripture and narrative texts. He could preach extemporaneously and quote long biblical passages like no one else I had ever met. What in particular he said over the course of the week escaped me, but it felt like he imparted a portion of his anointing to me in the manner of Elijah to Elisha. Rev. said he felt led to anoint attendees with oil at the conclusion of the week. This was the only occasion I recall of him doing so in my time there. Coincidentally, Rev. Durham died in the ensuing months.

Over the days following the revival, I prayed to God intensely for the something more that my heart was craving. I was awakened from a deep slumber around three o'clock in the morning the following week by a cataclysmic vision and an audible command to preach the gospel. It was akin to the prophet Isaiah's *woe is me* experience. Try as I might, I could not go back to sleep. I also could not focus at work over the next several weeks. A co-worker stopped by my office on several occasions and said I was glowing. I brushed her off by saying it was from riding with the moonroof of my car open. Shekinah glory cannot be hidden.

A snowstorm hit Washington, DC the first weekend of 1996, crippling the metropolitan area. I was on the telephone with a close friend that Saturday night as the snow began to fall. He could sense that I was not quite myself and withholding something. We talked for hours about everything under the sun except what was foremost in my mind. As the conversation dragged on, the snow continued to accumulate.

He noticed my recalcitrance and began interrogating me like he was pulling impacted wisdom teeth. I confessed for the first time that I was called to preach. The fact that I did so to him was a miracle in itself. He was prone to longwinded, patronizing advice, especially when I expressed vulnerability. He simply said "you have to go" and I felt unburdened. I always knew there was something special about our relationship.

We met four years prior when I was a year out of college. He was eight years my senior, dark chocolate, and handsome. We were attending a planning meeting at the Omega Psi Phi Fraternity house for a project co-sponsored by our respective graduate Chapters. After a couple hours of locking eyes, we exchanged numbers. He called me that same night. Ironically, our illicit intentions gave way to hours of discussing the gospel.

For the first time, I surrendered myself totally to God. Until then, everything about our relationship had to be on my terms. When I prayed, I thought I was seeking direction to join a ministry within the church or perform a discrete task. Never did it cross my mind that God wanted my whole life. Never had it crossed my mind either that I had not given it over already. I turned to my Bible and began reading it from cover to cover for the first time. Every waking hour my nose was in its pages. We were snowed in for over a week. I had almost finished the Bible by the time the roads became clear. This is a case in point that the call comes apart from redemption. I was not converted until afterward.

To my frustration and God's disappointment, I embarked upon the traditional path to institutionalized ministry. No other alternative crossed my mind. The first step was to subject myself to the AME Church's ordination process. It was initiated by informing Rev.

For reasons I did not recognize or understand at the time, Rev. opposed my pursuit of ministry. This is not speculation. The first thing he said when I informed him of my calling was, "you had better be glad I am not God because I would not have called you." I did not take offense because, quite frankly, I too thought God could have done better. In reality, this was Rev.'s first attempt to bring me down to the size he thought I should be. Everything he said to me until I disclosed my calling had been flattering. A good friend's mother who was pursuing ministry at a local Baptist church peeped Rev.'s game and pulled my coat on the peculiarity of the dynamic between us. As always, I was a slow learner and made excuses for his attention. God's anointing on me resulted in enmity between us.

Rev. put me to work as one of the youth minsters and gave me a level of engagement that I had never experienced before. Although I had no children of my own and was not particularly fond of them, I gave it my all. We had weekly Bible study, went on regular outings (at my expense or a favor from a friend), and became very close. I was at Rev.'s beck and call for a range of other responsibilities and cannot remember ever saying no. If he needed a ride to a meeting or someone to cover another Bible study, I was his go-to person. By this time, I averaged five to six days a week in church. Partying took a nosedive. It was less a matter of him controlling me than my willful assent. None of the requests at that point were unreasonable.

The next step was to preach before the congregation. Rev. delayed my initial sermon for almost nine months. Three newly minted ministers had just preached their initial sermons together a few months prior. He wanted to allow time for other candidates for licensure to be presented on the same program. That was fair because hosting an evening program was a considerable effort and expense. I did not take offense at the postponement because it allowed me to have one more summer of fun without the public persona of being a preacher. Don't judge me. I was in my twenties and living in a hip metropolis.

On the fourth Sunday of September 1996, I stood before a packed church. As the ministers gathered in the holding area, Rev. entered hurriedly asking "where did all these people come from?" I thought he was trying to psych me up because he did not think too many people would return for an evening program featuring a sole preacher who had not been a member of the congregation for long. The edifice was pretty large with a capacity of over 500. When I threw a date out, he readily accepted. Little did Rev. know it was my 28th birthday. (The date of my birth also happened to fall on the high holy Jewish holiday of Rosh Hashanah). I had a party in mind of a different order. God has orchestrated some form of sacrificial service for me every birthday since.

Taking the first step into the sanctuary brought me to tears. It was packed and the energy was high. Friends, family, Sorors, neighbors, co-workers, the party crew, and classmates from elementary through graduate school were in the building. My mother even invited the mailman. Looking over all those friendly faces was overwhelming. I sobbed all the way down the aisle and through the entire program. When the time came for me to preach, Rev. ordered the choir to sing another song because I was such an emotional wreck. Then I stood, with an amazing calm and confidence that I had a word from the Lord.

The next step was an oral examination by the Presiding Elder at the church's Quarterly Conference. He was pastor's supervisor and overseer of 42 churches in portions of DC, Maryland, and Northern Virginia as the leader of the Capital District. That meeting went off without a hitch because I had been spoon-fed the answers beforehand by ministers on staff. Rev. did not say much by way of introduction except that I had packed the church. In hindsight, his comment was a dog whistle signaling I must be stopped. The congregation voted unanimously to license me to preach and approve my advancement to the District Conference. Rev. took my license from the Presiding Elder and stored it in his office for "safekeeping." Mind you, I have never laid eyes on a license with my name on it to this day. Rev. told me "if anyone wants to confirm your licensure, tell them to call me." He did not do this to any other minister in the church.

Upon beginning the path toward ordained ministry, no one in leadership asked what I understood as my personal calling. I just performed what they defined as the necessary steps as did other candidates. The word "ministry" derives from the Hebrew term *misher* which means "to serve." What is my reasonable service in light of the gifts and graces with which God endowed me? The answer to that question is still unfolding as I meander on the long winding path to fulfilling my vocation.

The institutional church generally puts all prospects for the office on the same track whether they plan to pastor a church or not. Quite frankly, doing so does not suit my sensibilities. Some days, normal human interaction becomes a deterrent to productivity. I was willing to complete the process and accept an appointment if that was the price of the paper. Ironically, a dearth of positions is available for the thousands of ordination certificates issued annually.

Church officials made no overt mention that they were holding me back so I prepared for the next step, which was appearing before the District Conference led by the Presiding Elder. I requested leave from work for the week before Thanksgiving and bought a new suit. No one invited me to the conference personally, so I crashed it (as I am so wont to do). I drove nearly twenty miles to Union Bethel AME Church in Brandywine, Maryland each day and sat through the entire four-day proceedings without formal recognition. Rev. and the Presiding Elder were warm and cordial. The Presiding Elder even called me from those assembled to participate in leading the opening devotions with other licensed ministers. However, I was the only newly licensed minister in attendance who was not presented to the Board of Examiners. Life at Allen Chapel was subsequently business as usual.

The Washington Annual Conference followed in April of the next year. I got sharp as a tack to attend it as well. Thinking anyone would call my name for anything was preposterous being that the Board of Examiners at the District level recommends candidates for admission to the Annual Conference. I had fun nonetheless, hobnobbing with friends, ministers, and fellow churchgoers.

Members and non-members alike referred to Rev. flippantly as a pimp. Little did I know that Rev. really was a pimp. He was of average height, slight build, and ordinary looks. However, he had an affable personality, dressed sharply, and had a slick manner about him. I should have known something was amiss because it took almost a year for me to figure out which woman in the congregation was his wife. She was a lovely lady, but did not have top billing.

Rev's wife was not at all outgoing and lacked flash to match his. Members did not give her the same level of attention they offered him. I initially thought he was married to the woman who brought a homecooked dinner to his office every evening. Word on the street was his wife suffered multiple nervous breakdowns from the stress of his infidelity and emotional abuse. Unfortunately, that is not uncommon among pastors' wives as they work overtime to maintain a façade that most people see right through.

Rev. was known as the go-to man to line up women for any preacher passing through town, looking for something new on the side, or who simply could not get laid. An AME minister in another part of the country informed me that he must be the conference pimp, a common position throughout the denomination. What I thought was relationship-building over the past couple of years was grooming for vice.

Pastors of Rev's ilk are known to have a dedicated group of women who make themselves available howsoever requested. They get farmed out and passed around, then are discarded like a used tissue. The Lay Organization is a group of non-clergy AME members who train the laity on how to function in the church. The pastor's lay organization, as it was explained to me, consists of those who willingly offer themselves sexually as requested. This practice is not limited to the AME Church. The pastor of friend at a Baptist Church requested that she entertain a visiting revivalist each evening after service. She refused, but suffered no consequence as she was not pursuing ministry at the time.

So, what is the first thing a good pimp must do to a new addition to his stable? He must control her mind. He must play on her vulnerabilities. He must instill a constant sense of fear. And ultimately, he must get paid. I did not learn that in church; I learned that reading Iceberg Slim. Whatever the case, I knew the game, but did not know it was being played on me like that in God's house.

I did not need Rev.'s money or affirmation. The only thing he had to manipulate me was the piece of paper I then thought legitimized me as a preacher. For each time he assured me he was making special provisions for me to be ordained beyond the normal process, he also warned that I must play by his rules or suffer the consequences. For each time I offered to quit, he encouraged me to continue because otherwise it would have been game over.

My conflict with Rev. came to a head when I was applying to seminary. I knew I could not be focused at home in Washington, DC because I knew where trouble was and trouble was well acquainted with me. Rev. ordered me to remain local so he could keep an eye on me. I responded that I felt the Lord leading me away and invited him to be in prayer with me on the matter. To my surprise, he flat-out refused as if accountability was an offense. I had to return to the word which directs believers *do not believe every spirit, but test the spirits to see whether they are from God, because many false prophets have gone out into the world.* Rev. was amazed that I did not take his words as a command and went to great lengths to try to put me in my place.

The ensuing three years became an intense battle of the wills. Rev. ran that church like a heavy-handed dictator. Only now, I was no longer part of his regime. On one occasion, the congregation held a meeting to consider a financial matter Rev. proposed. He wanted Allen Chapel to co-sign a loan for the congregation of one of his protégés. The deliberations revealed a significant amount of unrest among the members. Rev. took the microphone before the vote and stated he would note each person's comments and position. Anyone opposing his will would consequently fall out of favor with him. The motion failed and he vowed to make good on his threat by blocking opportunities for those disapproving. Rev. was used to getting his way and became very vindictive when he did not.

The man who pretended to be my spiritual father could not handle that I, unlike many women around him, did not have a male void in my life as is common in the Black community. My father has always been an active presence in my life. Not even he could control my mind. I am also very close to my brother, who is next to me in birth order, and have many platonic male friends. However, Rev. found dissent with him disrespectful in itself. I started looking beyond his bespoke suits and acerbic wit to listening to Rev.'s sermons with my spiritual ear. Although he had good form, there was nothing but noise. I consequently began seeking spiritual direction and sustenance elsewhere.

To add insult to injury, I also defied the opportunities Rev. presented to hook up with men. Rev. sought me out on occasion at church-related events and worked the crowd with me in tow. I thought he was being a good mentor and helping me to socialize in the denomination. Nope.

He was showing off what he thought he could make available to the highest bidder. None of the men who approached me offered to take me anywhere nice or showed a genuine interest in me as a person. They all had one-track minds. When they saw they could not get anywhere with me sexually, they moved on to the next target. This was in addition to receiving calls from strange men assuming they could have sex with me, none of whom I ever gave my number. My refusal to play those games called Rev.'s pimping credentials into question.

I brought one of my best male friends to church with me a few times to satisfy speculation about my personal life. Rev. looked at me sternly and would not even speak to the young man when I tried to introduce them. Nevertheless, I had committed to celibacy at that point and thus I was off limits.

Being such an academic snob, I began to examine only top-tier theology programs around the country. The AME Church prides itself on requiring formal academic training in preparation for a career in ministry. I wanted to be among the best of them. Unfortunately, my congregation did not put its money where its mouth was. They never paid me a salary nor stipend for my services so it seemed reasonable to expect funding for equipping me professionally. Their lack of support did not deter me because God provides—even if that means selling one's soul to Sallie Mae.

Rev. sent a very glowing letter of recommendation in support of my application for theological studies. I should know because I wrote it at his request. The Presiding Elder promised to provide a letter of recommendation as well. I gave him the forms along with my resume and a summary of my church experience in November. The early deadline for scholarships was at the end of January. In the meantime, I called his secretary, reminded him during in-person encounters, included it in my reports to the Quarterly Conference, and did everything short of tree boxing him at home. He knew exactly what he was doing—in collusion with Rev.

The Presiding Elder eventually sent his letter of recommendation in April. Although I missed the opportunity to compete for the more generous scholarships, most of my tuition was underwritten by a scholarship endowed by the school's benefactors. My United Methodist classmates did not experience the same financial pressure. That denomination puts its money where its mouth is.

As the date of my departure for seminary drew nigh, Rev. became increasingly furious that I openly defied him. He confronted me directly about leaving town while in his office one evening as I was heading to Bible study. I responded, "I feel led by God to pursue my chosen path and have to wonder who is leading you?" He was not used to this type of straightforwardness as most ministers on staff kowtowed to him. It did not endear me to him any further, although the slights were subtle. Rev. never had any intention on helping me develop a sense of vocation. He simply wanted to guide me in catering to him. He was trying to whip me into submission mentally by chipping at my ego, withholding his usual compliments, or diminishing my ambitions outright. I flipped Rev. off mentally, while maintaining the optics of respecting his position.

In the weeks leading to my departure, Prince came to town to perform. I had been a fan since he first came on the scene in the late 70s—long before everybody liked him. The show conflicted with a youth ministry event. A few church members asked me to stop disclosing to the children why I was not going to be present because of the nature of the activity in which I would be engaging. They tried to make me feel guilty for going to see one whose music gave me life. Giving up the tickets was not an option because I camped outdoors overnight to buy them and I was not that holy yet. Many of his songs have underlying spiritual messages that are lost on the masses. Others are explicitly Christian and more theologically sound than what passes for gospel music today. However, that is not why I was going. I was going to get loose.

We dined at a restaurant nearby the Capital Centre before the concert. I kept pacing back and forth from the door to the reception area looking for the remainder of our party. On one trip, His Royal Badness' limousine was parked right outside the door. A friend later told me Prince passed through the lobby where I'd been standing after my party was seated. Good thing I did not come within close proximity of him because I would have likely fainted.

The show was everything and I do mean everything. He played hits from the beginning of his career up until that point in time. My mother is a bigger fan than me. Having married at 19, she did not have the opportunity for fun during her young adult years that I enjoyed. When Prince called for members of the audience to dance with him on stage, Mom darted down the aisle. I was in close pursuit and held her back because I could never live that down.

Still repressed by the church's admonitions, I tried to sit through a Prince concert with restraint. Imagine that. The Lord spoke to my heart saying, *So if the Son sets you free, you will be free indeed.* That released me to stop being a religious prig and boogie down for the rest of the night. My friends, mother, and I even lingered on the parking lot of the venue playing his CDs and partying with other diehard fans we met while camping outdoors for tickets. Prince would have been pleased that we stayed to see the dawn. One of my friends said "you have the coolest mother ever." When I dropped her off, Mom said "this was the best night of my life." When Prince passed almost twenty years later, I realized the experience of which I deprived her and apologized profusely. By no coincidence, his *Crystal Ball* album released after the concert had a song named after me pining "Dionne you could have been the one..."

The institutional church sometimes honors worldly accomplishment at the expense of spiritual growth. Following Rev.'s lead, several members of the congregation told me I did not need to pursue formal theological training. In their minds, I was smart enough and earned a sufficient living. Never mind that my previous education included absolutely no religious studies. It astounds me to this day to hear church folks marvel at what some have forsaken to pursue their respective callings as if the kingdom's work leaves something to be desired. As I prepared to leave for seminary, some warned me "don't let them steal your Jesus" as if the school was going to cut my heart out of my chest.

God directed me to the Candler School of Theology at Emory University through the prophetic word of a colleague in ministry. I only applied there despite requesting information packets from most of the top-ranked programs. It was confirmed when they extended an offer of admission almost immediately after my application was complete. Once

I got to Atlanta in August of 1997, my situation became one of out of sight out of mind. I found freedom pursuing my studies and believed obedience to God's direction would get me anything I wanted. All I wanted at this point was to be ordained and practice ministry. Most AME churches down there treated me like a marked woman when they realized I had neither a copy of my license nor pastoral endorsement. Warm embraces turned to cold shoulders on a dime.

My 29th birthday was within my first few weeks at Emory. In keeping with my personal tradition, I took myself out to a nice dinner in Buckhead to reflect and celebrate. A man approached me in the restaurant saying, "What's pretty young woman like you doing eating by herself?" I looked up and it was comedian George Wallace. He invited me to join his party and I accepted. We had a good time. The next day, he gave me a shout-out on the syndicated *Tom Joyner Morning Show* and wished me well in my pursuit of ministry. Members of Allen Chapel told Rev. He called me that evening asking why my name was mentioned on the radio. That was the only time he picked up the phone to check on me while I was away at seminary.

Nevertheless, I pressed onward. During my first year, I received no calls from Allen Chapel to return for conferences or to make arrangements to report there for any form of service during my breaks. Once I hit the road for Atlanta, I became a pariah in a sense. Having slow reflexes, I did not notice initially. However, the Bible study classes I adored became settings for challenging my theological training. The teens I served as youth minister were my consolation as they were not in step with church politics. They were, however, aware of Rev.'s character and remained a constant source of encouragement.

Ironically, the AME Church has one of the most educated clergy among Black denominations, requiring formal theological education for ordination to the itineracy. Allen Chapel did not plan to contribute anything to my education. Legendary civil rights attorney Dovey Roundtree—who was also on the ministerial staff—approached Rev. on the last Sunday prior to my departure. She said under no circumstances should the church send me away to school emptyhanded. Rev. grudgingly agreed to provide me with a one-time check for $500. The denomination also gave me $600 a semester, as it does all full-time seminarians. These contributions were a pittance of the overall cost of attending, not to mention their respective budgets.

This taught me a lot about how God works. As in Scripture, those with outwardly religious personas were the most lacking spiritually. My parents warned they would not foot the bill for my theological studies as they had put me through not one, but two, degree programs with their modest means. I respected their position and assured them smugly that God would make a way. Friends sent me checks during the school year and took me out to dinner when I came home during breaks while churchgoers watched passively as if they wanted to be spectators to my demise.

Rev. set the tone. He wanted me to fail due to my insubordination. However, he had no reach into the academic community to impede my progress like he did in the AME Church. I arrived at the Candler School of Theology wide open, but still fairly rigid. This was a monumental decision as Emory University has no Division I sports teams and is, suffice to say, rather tame socially. My mind engaged new theological concepts and biblical interpretation methods with glee. However, I had a spiritual chip on my shoulder defying anyone to try to alter my faith. One of my professors said I was one of the most combative students he ever had.

Without a doubt, I was prepared. I had read the Bible from beginning to end more than once, in addition to studying church history and theology. The writings of biblical scholar Renita Weems, father of liberation theology James Cone, and womanist theologian Jacqueline Grant were also familiar to me. Continuing the AME tradition of socially-conscious ministry was my goal. Learning about the African influence on the early church blew my mind. Until then, I had been told people of African descent were introduced to Christianity through slavery and colonialism. The oldest extant church in the world is located in Ethiopia, predating the Vatican See. Many theologians of the first few centuries were African like Athanasius, Origen, Tertullian, and Jerome. Paradoxically, the book we used to study the life of St. Augustine had a white image of him on the cover although he was from Algeria.

That excitement lasted exactly one semester. My second semester Christian History professor's syllabus was focused almost exclusively on dead white men. On top of that, he used slides of classic European works of art to complement theological concepts presented in class. Of course, they too were overwhelmingly white. On the one day allocated to Black Theology, he showed a picture of a Black Jesus and qualified it by disassociating the image from the historical figure. I interrupted him with a Buggin' Out moment from Spike Lee's movie *Do the Right Thing*. The professor was shocked to be challenged on his failure to do the same with the white images I had been resisting from seeping into my consciousness all semester. The power of promoting white imagery was not lost on him because he was a trained psychotherapist in addition to theologian. The professor offered to let me lecture one day if I could dredge up enough Black historical references and art to present alongside the course content. Imagine his surprise when I delivered to a standing ovation from the class without using resources beyond my personal library.

Every day I was there affirmed my decision to attend Emory. The faculty at the time was filled with rock stars in their respective areas that my friends at other schools only read about. As a matter of fact, Anglican Archbishop Desmond Tutu became a visiting professor while I was there. Our paths crossed on Tuesday and Thursday mornings as I departed my eight o'clock Hebrew class and he arrived to teach his 9:30 course. I rushed to open the door all starstruck one morning as he approached saying, "let me get that for you." He sped to hold it for me replying, "I am still a man."

We had mid-day worship services during the week and some instructors included opening devotions in their lesson plans. The course offerings met my every established and emerging interest. There was no mistaking that they took training ministers seriously. It was ranked one of the top five programs not only in the United States, but in the world, when I attended. We had classmates from all over Africa, East Asia, Western Europe, and of course the United States.

One of my closest classmates came from Angola in southwest Africa. He learned English only five months prior to matriculating with us and eventually rocked his studies after a slow start. I received a first-hand lesson in colonialism and imperialism from him. Most tellingly, I asked what color the pictures of Jesus would be in his church back home. He rolled his eyes and said, "you know."

One day while we were riding in my car, he expressed how tormented he was by all the lives he took. "What lives?!!" I exclaimed. He grew up under Portuguese rule and served as a Soviet-trained soldier during his country's Civil War against American supported troops. All those years of watching reports of the Rebels in Angola on *60 Minutes* finally had real context. Studying theology helped him on a personal journey with some heavy issues as he prepared for a new career in pastoral ministry and eventual American citizenship.

Homesickness began to set in toward the end of my first semester. Attending college only a stone's throw from home was not really like being away. Duke was less than four hours away and I came home frequently for the weekend. That nine-and-a-half-hour drive to Atlanta kept me stuck. I also did not have any close friends or family there. As Thanksgiving approached, I realized I had been away from home for the longest time ever. It was also the first time I was not able to travel home for the holiday. A classmate found it unacceptable that I planned to dine alone and invited me to his family's festivities. I had the best Thanksgiving meal ever and they sent me home with enough food for a week.

Seminary exposed me to my first experience of the Eucharist by intinction. The celebrant held a whole loaf high, broke it in half, and tore a piece to serve each participant. Another celebrant held a chalice of wine in which each participant dipped their portion. For the first time, I truly felt part of something not only immensely beyond my comprehension, but also in solidarity with those engaging the observance with me. True to form, I cried like a baby and was in good company with others who shared those feelings.

It was a wonderful way to initiate those of us who were entering a new phase of life filled with mystery of how God would form us anew and use us to advance the redemption of the world. The broken bread was a stark reminder that Jesus gave Himself to be persecuted and killed at the hands of men. What sacrifices would we endure? The potency of the wine conveyed the power of his blood to forgive sin—our own as well as that of the world. The wine itself was a surprise because quite some time had passed since churches of my denomination replaced it with watered-down grape juice.

There was no temptation for me in Atlanta. That was important because I did not know how strong my newfound resolve with abstinence was. I was on a mission, so I was not cruising among my classmates or church members. Fortunately, a good share of my classmates shared the same mindset. The population of gay men in Atlanta is also larger than is widely held. The resulting proportion of eligible, datable Black men to Black women presented a woeful imbalance of power in dating dynamics. It is not uncommon to see sisters there involved in full-fledged relationships with men who should not even know their government names. Crossing racial lines romantically is not beyond my scope, but not terribly common in those parts. From day one, I knew it would be a long three years.

Early in the semester, a Black female professor hosted a fellowship at her home for Black women seminarians. It was a wonderful sight to see about forty of us gathered for what was known as "Sisters' Circle" in her well-appointed suburban home. We shared our personal stories and upperclassmen provided words of encouragement. I did not want to dampen the mood, but I kept it real when my turn came. It felt good to be embraced and know there were others who understood my experience.

The conversation then shifted to accounts of scandals and women struggling in the broader church that were far more salacious than mine. I was supposed to count myself as blessed that sexual harassment was all I was experiencing. Being that my parents did not attend church, I was never privy to insider information growing up. Although my participation increased significantly leading up to ministry, I still maintained what I considered a healthy professional distance from parishioners. What I was hearing was horrifying. There were stories of adulterous affairs, rapes, forced abortions, embezzlement, closet homosexuality, and intimate partner violence by high profile ministers. My repulsion was tempered by the professor stating how influential and connected she was in our denomination. She offered to intervene with senior officials in the AME Church on my behalf if I so desired. It felt good to have an ace in the hole.

Knowing people who are well-acquainted with the plight of those who have experienced the persistent hypocrisy of the church, yet have the gall to criticize us for being angry, continues to astound me.

They share gossip like it is a trophy, but assume no accountability for its consequences. Jesus said *Is it not written: "My house will be called a house of prayer for all nations?" But you have made it a den of thieves.* Our Lord and Savior was not particularly happy when he said this about the defilement of the temple and can in no way be happy about the state of the modern church.

I visited all of the AME churches within close proximity to Emory University. Pastors and parishioners alike treated me with suspicion when their inquiries into my status were not answered to their satisfaction. Rev. implied that he knew nothing of which they spoke when receiving calls about me. The sacrifice I was making to pursue theological education did not matter to them without the endorsement of institutional leaders. This made me wonder why I was caring so much about serving those who did not care at all about me.

Not one to be deterred, I went for broke incurring student loans for the remainder of my tuition and my living expenses. What I thought were substantial savings disappeared before the end of my first year. The sunk financial and opportunity costs had me in too deep to quit. Forging ahead was all I could do not to lose my mind over the direct and indirect costs of pursuing theological training. Fortunately, I was able to earn decent money during the summers applying my prior experience at corporations around metropolitan Atlanta.

It bothered me to no end that nobody in the organized church cared that God's gifts and investments were going to waste. (The freedom of my ministry being unencumbered by organizational constraints had not sunk in yet). Members of Allen Chapel watched conference after conference pass without me progressing in the ordination process. Not one person raised a question although they knew me well. People at St. Philip, the AME church with which I affiliated in Atlanta, knew I was a training to become a minister, but had no problem with me sitting idly among the laity. Meanwhile, my classmates were invariably being trained in their respective congregations without any barriers.

Uncharacteristically, I did not question my unfruitful engagement of this process. Scripture posits, *And how can they hear without someone preaching to them? And how can anyone preach unless they are sent?* The only human action necessary for the execution of a call to ministry is acceptance of the call. A simple "yes" would do. No pomp and pageantry, no jumping through hoops, not even hallowed degrees (clutch the pearls) are required to preach. To do so well does require faith, discernment, consecration, and obedience. Education is an enabler of effective ministry, but does not make up for a deficiency of the call itself. Playing along mindlessly was so atypical for me. I love being the renegade, the contrarian, the eccentric—my own woman.

This experience did not deter me from wanting to remain committed to the institution. As a matter of fact, I concealed my struggle and defended the church fiercely. Corporate worship renews my soul in a way that spectating remotely does not. So, I started randomly attending churches around town in Atlanta after I eventually left the AME Church and in DC upon returning home after graduation.

Some Sundays, getting dressed was my only motivation to go to church. During the depths of my disillusionment, only a newly acquired outfit stood between "Bedside Baptist" or "Pillow Pentecostal" and a place of collective worship. Not proud of that fact, but at least it got me into the house of the Lord.

There are some people whose gift it is to reveal that if nothing else is working right in the world, it is the ensemble they have pulled together. Every church has at least one sister or brother who worships God with sartorial splendor. Everybody brings something to the body. If strutting on the ecclesiastical red carpet is your gift, own it.

> *And why do you worry about clothes? See how the flowers of the field grow. They do not labor or spin. Yet I tell you that not even Solomon in all his splendor was dressed like one of these. If that is how God clothes the grass of the field, which is here today and tomorrow is thrown into the fire, will he not much more clothe you—you of little faith?*

One of my closest sisters in ministry definitely had that anointing. Angelia showed up on the first day of seminary like she was walking the runway. Everybody looked at her wondering where she thought she was going. She never let shady attitudes disrupt her shine and continued to carry herself just as stylish as she was when God called her. Angelia was probably the only person in the entire building for whom it was not out of character to rock cutting-edge fashions, designer stilettos, and a full face of make-up every day. She stepped her look up more on Sunday mornings and even more so as she endured a debilitating struggle with lupus.

God wants God's people to look good and especially good for the sake of the kingdom. Tradition holds that believers began putting on their best on Sundays in honor of the angels who were present at the empty tomb after Jesus' resurrection. They have been described in some translations of Luke 24:4 as *wearing dazzling clothes*. What better occasion to look your best than when meeting God incarnate face-to-face?

That is what Sunday mornings represent. Yes, God is present everywhere at all times. But the assembly of the saints for the purpose of hearing what thus sayeth The Lord is a personal presentation. Jesus himself encourages us to keep up our appearances.

> *When you fast, do not look somber as the hypocrites do, for they disfigure their faces to show others they are fasting. Truly I tell you, they have received their reward in full. But when you fast, put oil on your head and wash your face, so that it will not be obvious to others that you are fasting, but only to your Father, who is unseen; and your Father, who sees what is done in secret, will reward you.*

Blessed are those who can keep it together no matter what they are going through. One of the most iconic pictures in American history is of Jacqueline Kennedy mourning at her husband's funeral. Even in her grief, she was giving it up with the same elegance she had always been known for exhibiting.

So, I sat through worship Sunday after Sunday during the height of my struggle trying to hold it together. I went to great lengths to ensure my hair, clothes, and makeup were tight while I was unraveling inside. I would enter church and greet everyone enthusiastically. Then, I would go to the pastor's office and show him some love. Rev. acted as if we were on the best of terms and not engaged in intense warfare while others were present. The choir, ministers, and acolytes would proceed into the sanctuary to launch the dog and pony show. Some days, I could barely make it through service without being reduced to tears.

Almost every sister in ministry I know can recount a time or twenty when she has felt the same way. I have had the privilege of functioning as a member of the ministerial staff, but it was only symbolic. Others have been ordained for years while watching less qualified men receive coveted positions. Yet, we play along with the vain hope that we can get ours and the game will change on its own.

3

THE GAME

Keep the faith. Don't keep the secrets.

Jill Nelson

We were in the fourth quarter and I had just realized there was a game. In the parlance of the streets, if you are just recognizing the game, you have already lost. Rev. had run up the score on me and my odds of winning were slim to none. Getting points on the board required me to move in silence. Little did I know, the fix was in for me never to be ordained by human hands.

Rev. operated straight from the manual of hustling authored by none other than Iceberg Slim. *Pimp: The Story of My Life* has served as the playbook for many brothers coming into their own. He did not invent the game, but rather codified it for the modern era. As a matter of fact, Kierkegaard described how men manipulate women in *The Seducer's Diary*. Many Black men have adopted Iceberg Slim's characterization of a pimp as their root metaphor whether they are involved in vice or just navigating the more routine paths of life. Iceberg Slim repented later in life, acknowledging the pathology of his ways. However, the horse was too far out of the barn by then.

I dated a man in graduate school whose entire worldview was shaped by pimping. He could quote Iceberg Slim's writings by chapter and verse and knew every detail of the 1970s blaxploitation movie *The Mack*. He was handsome, well-dressed, very intelligent, and knew how to show a dame a good time. His reputation with the ladies preceded him. One of his fraternity brothers even broke code and strongly suggested I not consort with him. Why I thought getting involved with such a person was a good idea is beyond me.

The relationship started well with all the requirements of romance on my end and seduction on his. He said womanizing was behind him, true to the game. His slavish adherence to its principles was purportedly due to the universality of its rules. He was in law school at the University of North Carolina and claimed to be aspiring to more honorable pursuits. What he passed off as smitten attention was actually a device of the game—social isolation—to keep me unaware of his chain of fools. One of my few real friends on campus brought the truth to me while many so-called ones gossiped behind my back.

I was more crushed that I bought his excuses than at experiencing my first real heartbreak. After the saga was over, I read his bible and revisited the film I did not quite comprehend when I watched it as a child. The universe taught me the lessons of the game twice more until I stopped repeating the error of my ways.

The pimp establishes his position first by dazzling onlookers with his appearance. In other words, he must look the part. Rev.'s attire stood out upon our first meeting, although it was not ostentatious. He drove an old minivan and wore a conventional close-cropped haircut—not the premium automobile and stylized coiffure of street pimps.

However, his suits were conservative and well-tailored. Each seam, dart, and hem hit his body exactly where they should. The lines of the fabric's patterns aligned perfectly. His shirts were custom made with his initials embroidered on the cuff. His ties were premium silk. His shoes were always clean, shined, and looked barely worn. I and others complimented him frequently on how he assembled his ensembles. He would return the favor if one were wearing something that caught his eye.

Rev. projected an image of success as the pastor of the largest AME congregation in Washington, DC at the time. He also had over a dozen ministers on staff, although most were not compensated. Each had assigned duties in the life of the church and rotated as backup preachers.

The vast majority were female. The males acted like eunuchs to Rev.'s alpha male, save for one or two. Collectively, this made for the appearance of an impressive stable.

Pimps were frequent sights in the city when I was coming of age. The corner of 14th and U Streets Northwest was their headquarters as the center of one of DC's most notorious red-light districts. I once met a real live pimp as a young woman while stopping at Ben's Chili Bowl after a night of clubbing. His identity was clear at first glance. He wore a garish suit, excessive jewelry, and exhibited all the stereotypical mannerisms. He glided toward my friends and me while we waited to place our orders. They turned their backs while I decided to humor him.

The pimp leaned one elbow on the counter and faced me.

"Hey baby! How you doin'?"

I gave a restrained smile trying not to burst out laughing. "I'm fine, thanks."

"Say, can I buy you something to eat?"

"No, thank you."

"So, what's a nice girl like you doing up in here at this hour?"

"On my way home. I come from a very good home."

The waitress pushed greasy bags of food across the counter shouting order numbers in the midst of our back-and-forth banter. My girls and I grabbed ours and bolted for the door giggling.

The over-accessorized Cadillac parked outside confirmed our assumptions. The night was over for us while it was in full swing for him. The one thing I had in my favor was I did not need anything. The conversation did not last long enough for the pimp to probe for my Achilles heel as predators do with their prey. Very seldom will a pimp approach a runaway in a bus station and announce he wants to enlist her in sex trafficking. He first meets her immediate needs. The tricking and abuse come later.

Grooming is the first step in the process. It begins with disarming the target with flattery, generosity, and unfettered affection. The pimp has got to make his mark feel special. He becomes not only the primary source of her self-esteem, but also her security. Goldie—the protagonist of *The Mack*—lays it on thick with a prospect "You've got to believe in me. You've got to believe everything I tell you to do is for the best." Mind you, he never tells her his line of work or his plans for her life up front.

Likewise, Rev. never informed me he was one of the main traffickers of women in the AME Church while he ingratiated himself to me. He behaved initially as the fatherly figure he was. This was quite the diversion having grown up with a cold, distant relationship with my pastor and congregation. He listened intently to everything this spiritual runaway said to identify my weaknesses. He also ensured the congregation embraced me. Rev. was always complimentary, warm, and jovial—until he wasn't. Rev. always made me feel like an insider—until he didn't. A pimp does not reveal much about himself to maintain an air of mystery. To this day, I still do not know much about Rev. despite our frequent interactions.

Announcing my call to ministry presented a definite shift in our relationship, although my entrance into the realm of the consecrated did not change Rev.'s intentions. Our rapport turned on a dime going from the affection of the initial meeting to the callousness of the stroll. The tension between the spiritual seeker and carnal exploiter was hard to endure.

Grooming is targeted not only at the objects of prey, but also at everyone whose support the predator needs—either actively or passively. In the context of the streets, a pimp needs to instill fear in anyone who might interfere with his game. That includes his stable, johns, competitors, and law enforcement. On the other hand, he must also cultivate loyalty from the same crowd through benefits of the trade. Rev. maintained a well-oiled machine run by church members who kept the surface operation going. Any negative statements about him were conveyed as a threat to the entire enterprise. People were free to disagree with him, but the machine must be kept grinding with continuous affirmation. Rev. had an air of authority that inspired deference in the broader community. His superiors also refused to check him. Even when he was wrong, he was right because the show had to go on and bills had to be paid.

Initiation is the next step in the process. It reveals the true purpose of the relationship to the prey. Grooming is intended to seal the identities and dynamics within that relationship. Any disruption caused by the revelation is redirected by the mind control instilled during grooming.

When a woman is shocked when a man moves the boundaries of their relationship by asking her to sell her body, he resorts to the supposed love they share and how good he has been to her. She is usually powerless to resist even when he attacks her violently for coming up short with his money.

Initiation is seldom announced, just introduced in the moment. I had no idea Rev. cultivated a warm relationship with me as inducement to perform sexual favors for him. He also established a consistent dynamic of call and response by making frequent requests and keeping me busy around the church. Likewise, a pimp seldom tells a new prospect what his designs are while he is showering her with compliments, lavishing her with gifts, and wining and dining her. She is just thrown into the pool without warning as was I.

It was not until we attended the Washington Annual Conference the April following my announcement of my call to ministry that I realized the game Rev. was playing. I heard people young and old often refer to him as a pimp, but assumed it was a figure of speech. Therefore, I joined the chorus. He was far from the caricature, but fit the mold perfectly. His tactics were straight from the street. Each time he approached me after a male minister's failed attempts to connect with me sexually, he would appeal with classic manipulation.

"You're making me look bad. Come on! Do this for me." He pleaded.

"No!"

"People will say you are a lesbian if you don't go out with any of them."

"There is far too much evidence to the contrary from my past for me to feel threatened" I said as I turned and walked away.

"I thought you were loyal," he sneered.

"You done lost your mind," I whispered under my breath.

In the midst of it all, a pimp must maintain control. He needs to know where his workers are at all times. He keeps his ear to the ground for intel. He keeps his stable dependent on him financially, psychologically, and physically. Although the church was deep in the 'hood, members were safe from the crime surrounding it because of the respect Rev. commanded. His first reaction to my announcement of a call to ministry was an attempt to chop me down. "You had better be glad I am not God because I would not have called you." That was the equivalent of pimp slap.

Soon thereafter, Rev. gave me the opportunity to feel special. He summonsed me to give one of the denomination's bishops a ride to the airport as we were leaving my childhood pastor's funeral telling him I was one of his best girls. It was not an imposition as I was not going to the cemetery anyway. The bishop was a nice man and very accessible in conversation. We discussed my plans for ministry and his plans for retirement during the relatively short ride. He asked me to take him somewhere nice to grab a quick bite to eat before his flight. We had lunch at a restaurant where the firm I worked frequently hosted corporate events and clients. He paid.

When I dropped the bishop off at the terminal, he pressed a crisp, folded one-hundred-dollar bill wrapped around his business card in my palm. I did not even recognize what type of bill it was because the Department of the Treasury had just changed its appearance with the enlarged portrait of Benjamin Franklin and new security features. He refused my attempt to return it stating that it was "funny money." "Stay in touch and there will be more where that came from."

When I went to church later that evening, Rev. requested a full report. He was irate to learn of my experience with the bishop. Rev. now regretted connecting me with a bigger fish than him. He took the business card. "You don't want to be travelling in those circles. Besides, it will cost me $10,000 a visit to have a bishop walk through the doors of this church." I did not tell Rev. about the money. The bishop and I had no further contact.

Rev. made sure the women on the ministerial staff did not get too close. He would talk about the others to me as I am sure he did about me to them. Rev. would greet me as I entered the church. He insisted I check in with him in his office if he was not visible upon my entrance. He also required me to inform him if I planned to deviate from my normal routine.

Rev. also tried to employ me to spy on others for him. When the women of the church returned from our annual retreat, he asked me for a rundown on everything that occurred including the content of teachings. I told him nothing of significance. He warned against getting caught up in feminism and referred to the guest preacher as a witch. I laughed it off.

He maintained constant control of my pursuit of ordained ministry throughout the process and it became more intense as time passed. Rev.'s first tactic was telling me he would not have called me to ministry as if he had the authority. That was a power play for me to seek his approval, which I never did. Secondly, he delayed my initial sermon by nine months to convey the message that I was not ready until he said I was ready. It was nothing for the church to plan an unscheduled service for the most inconsequential event. Never mind he did absolutely nothing to help me prepare my message or provide any type of positive mentorship. I had to sink or swim on my own. Third, his introduction during the program did not say much about me personally, but was more of an announcement to those assembled—including members of my former congregation—that I belonged to him now. From his perspective, I had chosen my pimp.

Next, Rev. kept my license to preach under lock and key, refusing to provide copies to ministers at other churches wanting to confirm my status. The pastor of the AME Church I attended regularly in Atlanta sought to bypass Rev. and get me ordained discreetly while I was away at school. Rev. made calls to make sure no other conference approved me. The Atlanta pastor dared not violate the game by going against another pastor of equal standing. Ultimately, Rev. expressed his sense of control by blacklisting me and impeding my progress in ministry in the denomination and beyond.

In March 2017, an older male neighbor beckoned me to assist a young lady crumpled in a heap against the base of a lamppost. She was tall, thin, and pretty with long braided extensions. Her inebriated state betrayed the innocence of her face. I was walking my dog between games of the second round of the NCAA men's basketball tournament and had no interest in being a hero. March Madness is my high holy season. My neighbor seemed to know what the situation was as well as his limitations for intervening. I saw myself in her and then felt compelled to be a Good Samaritan.

"What's the matter young lady?" I asked.

"My boyfriend got me drunk and began making strange demands. He put me out because I would not have sex with a man he invited over. I have never consumed alcohol before."

"How old are you?"

"Fifteen."

"I'm taking you home. Where do you live?"

"I don't want to go home like this. My mother will be mad."

"OK, you're going home with me. It's either there or the police station."

"I'll go home with you."

I allowed her to lean her long, slender frame on me as she struggled to walk a single city block. Before we even got to my house, her "boyfriend" began blowing up her mobile phone. I answered when we got inside and informed him I would neither disclose where she was nor return her to him. He was furious over losing control of the situation now that she had an advocate. I sat across from her at my dining room table.

"Just how old is your boyfriend?" I asked.

"Twenty-eight."

"Has he ever offered you to another man before?"

"No. I thought he loved me. We have sex all the time. He promised me our relationship was special."

"Relationship? What did he buy you for Valentine's Day?"

She looked startled and whispered, "Nothing."

"Where has he taken you on dates? You do know that's what boyfriends do."

"Nowhere. We just go to his apartment and have sex. We talk on the phone and text a lot. And he gives me money."

"Have you met his mother?"

"No."

"That doesn't sound like much of a relationship. Boyfriends don't make you have sex with other men."

"I know…but he said he loves me." she replied sheepishly.

I rose from my chair, held her by the shoulders, and gave her a long cold stare. She started crying from the realization that the romance was a lie. I hugged her tightly.

"Let me get something to sober you up so we can take you home." Her phone was ringing almost non-stop on the living room mantel. When I went to turn down the guest room bed for her, she fled through the front door screaming his name. MIIIICHAEL!!!

Indifference is the hallmark of a good pimp. The most successful pimps show the least emotions. Iceberg Slim stated in his autobiography that he earned his nickname because his heart was cold as ice. According to legend, someone shot a bullet through the top of his hat while he sat at a bar and he did not flinch. In *The Mack*, Goldie confronts his most trusted prostitute as she is running for her life from an angry john. "Listen to me and you listen to me closely. I don't give a shit about what happened to you. Now I want you to get yourself together; get back out there; and get me my money."

Each member of the church represented a revenue stream to Rev. My leaving the workforce for full-time theological studies represented the loss of not only one giving unit, but also a source of free labor. He never empathized as he watched me suffer in my striving. As a matter of fact, Rev. relished my financial struggles as an opportunity to bend my will. But I never relented. His indifference toward me personally did not bother me as much as his indifference toward my success in ministry. The latter was quite telling about where he stood with God.

In the final analysis, almost everything in life is a game—even in the church, especially in the church. One must go through life with this recognition or continue getting played. According to Iceberg Slim, pimping is not a sex game; it's a mind game. Most pimping in the church, secular institutions, and interpersonal relationships does not involve sex. It involves controlling thoughts so people will do exactly what is profitable and beneficial to those in power. My leaving the church was an abandonment of the game, but with my faith intact.

I had to write this for those still trapped in the game. Either they are totally unaware, silenced by their ambitions, or walk around blissfully ignorant so they do not have to be inconvenienced by reforming the settings of the offenses. The first group was most compelling as I wish a book like this existed while I walked around the church blindly. Communities of faith are assumed to be safe spaces. Nothing could be further from the truth. That level of naiveté about the institution marks one as prey.

We must gird ourselves up to *be as shrewd as serpents and as innocent as doves*. The spiritual journey is not easy. Growth requires pain and sacrifice. Defend your integrity and honor as if your life depended on it. You will have to fight even when you do not perceive yourself on enemy territory. Sociopaths cloak themselves in good works to provide onlookers with plausible deniability when accusations surface. Teachings in the church usually point to an enemy outside its boundaries while adherents drop their guard against the ones within. For the most part, no one is hipping believers to the game.

The second group is the most culpable. I was a part of it for a brief season while initially seeking ordination. This includes those who actively participate in exploiting and concealing to those who gossip about wrongdoing while doing nothing to correct it. Watching women praise no-good preachers to the highest heaven just for the opportunity to build their own platforms within patriarchy pains me. These same women are the main spillers of tea. Prominent male ministers are just as aware of the game being run in the church. Never have I heard one rebuke it during addresses to large assemblies of preachers. Becoming dumb for the sake of preserving one's share of the spoils makes them just as guilty. Abuse continues. Meanwhile, the institution rewards them richly for their continued allegiance as they bask in the pomp and pageantry of their façade of holiness.

The third group has an idea the game exists, but has developed a blind spot for their comfort. "I don't know and I don't want to know" is their prevailing sentiment. This attitude breeds inertia in the body as the things that offend God become palatable to people calling themselves God's own. In the meantime, people suffer. As a matter of fact, the entire body of Christ suffers. *Do not be deceived: God cannot be mocked. A man reaps what he sows.* God will raise a critical mass to remove the rot from God's house. You are either part of the problem or part of the solution. There are no two ways about it. Those who are contributing to the problem are hereby on notice.

4

METHOD TO THE MADNESS

The chains of habit are generally too small to be felt until they are too strong to be broken.

Samuel Johnson

R egular church attendance was such a powerful habit that it felt embedded in my DNA. Regardless of how I felt about the institution, it was the first thing on my mind as I awakened every Sunday. I had to consciously plan to do something else as my mind would be deciding which dress to wear and what to eat for breakfast before I could even rise from my bed.

Behavioral scientists have identified three key aspects of habit formation: cue, response, and reward. Environmental stimuli lead us to engage in a certain behavior that produces a desired outcome. Charles Duhigg presents a series of compelling case studies in his best-selling book *The Power of Habit* to illustrate this model. "Habits are powerful, but delicate. They can emerge outside our consciousness, or can be deliberately designed.[3]

In one set of experiments, researchers trained mice to press levers in response to certain cues until the behavior became a habit. The mice were always rewarded with food. Then the scientists poisoned the food so it made the animals violently ill or electrified the floor so when the mice walked toward their reward, they received a shock. The mice knew the food and cage were dangerous—when offered the poisoned pellets in a bowl or the electrified floor panels, they stayed away. When they saw their old cues, however they unthinkingly pressed the lever and ate the food, or they walked across the floor, even as they vomited or jumped from the electricity. The habit was so ingrained the mice couldn't stop themselves.[4]

That explains the method to my madness. It seemed like I could not go long without being in community with fellow believers. When things fell apart as a result of Rev.'s sexual harassment and the congregation's indifference, the last thing I wanted to do at the time was attend church. I would workout at the gym, walk my dog, take long-distance bicycle rides, visit museums, watch grass grow—anything but go to church. Joining another congregation was out of the question at this point as the wounds were still raw.

But there are some dresses that are too fancy for work and not enough for after-five. Where would I wear them? Seriously, I loved praising God and studying the Word. But what was passing for church became revolting. I could not tell whether my motivation to go to church was temporal or divine. Theologically speaking, it was akin to St. Augustine's cry. "O Lord our hearts are restless until it finds rest in you."[5] I tried with all my might to put my calling to sleep to no avail.

Avoiding worship service was not enough to free me. I broke my five-year stint with celibacy and had a series of ill-advised relationships. They all ended badly and landed me in the realm of regret. Of course, I bargained with God to get me out of each mess before I killed someone with the promise that I would never do such again.

Then God revealed there is no requirement to attend church. Every. Single. Sunday. Yes, the Bible says *not [to forsake] our own assembling together, as is the habit of some.* That passage was written to a community in distress as they were under persecution for their faith. It was not, however, a prescription for overdosing on organized religion. Society has misconstrued the primary function of Christianity as assembled public worship as opposed to serving and discipling the world.

Duhigg's second point was that unless you deliberately fight a habit—unless you find new routines—the pattern will unfold automatically. True to form, I gave up skipping church for Lent the season following my graduation from seminary. One Saturday, God directed me to attend a historic United Methodist Church in downtown DC. I had spent most of my life working and shopping nearby without ever giving it a second look. So, I went and felt something I had not felt in a long time. My soul was nourished and I got my mojo back. Without deliberation, I went again, and again, and again. The God from whom I had been estranged started revealing things to me like before. However, I had no intention on joining and being the same fool twice.

As soon as I entered the sanctuary, I knew I had found a new spiritual home. The worship style and cast of characters had a strange familiarity. "The doctrine and polity of the [AME] church, set forth in The Book of Discipline, were modeled after the original Methodist Episcopal Church, as was the case with other Black Methodist bodies."[6] Richard Allen and Absalom Jones actually founded a nondenominational mutual aid society in 1787 to advance religious autonomy for people of African descent in America. They each founded separate Black denominations patterned after white ones only after a schism erupted between them. I can only imagine how different the Black church experience and impact in America would have been had we reimagined faith in light of our communal African heritage rather than creating facsimiles of Eurocentric practices of Christianity.

Although almost all the faces at my new church were Black, but there was no mistaking this congregation subscribed to the white brand of Methodism. Yes, African Methodism has no shortage of white Jesuses. However, Black United Methodist churches tend to seem even more colonized. While my childhood church was more aspirational, these people had arrived for the most part. Respectability was the aim with this crowd. Although the church was founded by Blacks who left the predominantly white Foundry Methodist Episcopal Church within walking distance due to discrimination, it was organized and underwritten by the denomination's leaders. The huge stained-glass window with a white image traditionally held to be Jesus over the entrance is emblematic of that.

The members were almost identical to my childhood church with the exception of their deeper roots. The formation of the new congregation pre-dates the Civil War. Several of its families go back several generations as native Washingtonians and as members. It was named "Asbury" after one of the first bishops of the Methodist Church. (Of course, he was white). Many long-time members were directed there upon moving to the nation's capital seeking economic opportunities not available to them in the South. They even had over a dozen centenarians. I had never met anyone over one-hundred years of age before joining Asbury. I was a baby to them at 32 with the average age there being almost 70. Although they have a history as a well-educated, silk-stocking crowd, their rapidly declining membership jeopardizes that.

The membership included some high-profile government and business leaders. That impressed me less than the fact that people experiencing homelessness felt welcome to worship alongside them. It was not unusual to see unhoused neighbors seated during service and embraced as brothers and sisters. Asbury also had a robust outreach program for them. Nevertheless, I still resisted taking that walk down the aisle during the invitation. But the monkey was riding my back. I had dresses to wear, songs to sing, and people to meet.

As I exited the church on the second Sunday I attended, the pastor greeted me by name. It was jarring, as most pastors tend to keep their distance until forced not to do so. One day when I was just out of college, I passed Rev. Robinson on the streets of downtown DC while on my lunchbreak from work. I stopped in my tracks and greeted him excitedly as if he were the Crown Prince of Zamunda. He looked terrified like I was a complete stranger about to assault him. Mind you, I was still a member of his church and had been shaking his hand every Sunday after service for years as I lied about how life-changing his sermon was. (That's why they call it the liar's line).

Then it became apparent that my lack of family ties within the congregation and meager monetary contributions made me just another face in the crowd. Forget what the Bible says about a good shepherd knowing his sheep by name. He did not even oversee a mega church— just a few hundred souls. Rev. Robinson passed away about five years later. At his wake, Rev. Walter L. Hildebrand, his predecessor who had been promoted to Presiding Elder, looked at me with a sense of recognition. He left Ward when I was in the fourth grade, but knew my essence.

"Remind me of your name," he said gently. "Can't say that I know you personally, but I know you are one of mine. You see the eyes are the windows to the soul." My heart melted from learning someone claimed me spiritually. Unfortunately, he too passed away soon thereafter.

The fact that Rev. Matthews remembered my name after a single encounter spoke volumes. His parishioners were not mere objects, but real beings over whose spiritual well-being he demonstrated stewardship. I continued attending for a year without any plan to join this or any other church. But my spirit was yearning for a resting place. I called the church secretary to schedule a meeting to interview the pastor for the job of being mine. Rev. Matthews said wryly "Either you're going to join the church or you're not. I am clearly qualified." We both had a good laugh and I became a member of Asbury United Methodist Church in February of 2002.

I told Rev. Matthews I knew almost every scandalous preacher in town and none knew him personally. That was a sterling endorsement of his character. He began to inquire about my spiritual journey. I had to pinch myself as the only other time this ever came up was during my seminary application. We had a series of subsequent sessions during which I shared my full story. His heart ached as he learned of my travails. Rev. Matthews received me well, nursed me back to health spiritually, and assured me of safety under his watch. Through all our meetings, his wife, who sat outside his door as the church secretary, never raised an eyebrow. Although I bared my soul, he never uttered a word of those sessions. His wife treats me like a daughter to this day. I love them both to pieces.

Regular attendance and financial contributions were not sufficient for Rev. Matthews. He allowed me to flex my gifts of teaching and preaching without reservation AND entered my name into candidacy for ordained ministry. I had been teaching Bible study or Vacation Bible School for over a decade at this point and had high marks on my seminary transcript (which I had mailed to him from the university to verify my claims). However, I could not get a job as a substitute Sunday School teacher because Rev. had blacklisted me thoroughly. If he had not done so overtly, simply his refusal to endorse me was a tacit sign that I was not to be accepted.

By some stroke of fate, I got laid off three weeks after closing on my new house. Surprisingly, I never panicked. A strange sense of calm came over me indicating it was another part of God's plan. The terrorist attacks of September 11, 2001 occurred three months before I bought my house. My government contract was cut to reallocate funds to the ensuing wars. The homebuyers' program I used did not require a down payment for my mortgage. Therefore, I was able to live off my savings and severance while I took a sabbatical to work in the church and decorate my home.

Being in the Nation's Capital during the months following the events of 9-11—observing soldiers on the corner holding assault rifles, tanks driving down the street, and fighter jets flying overhead—had begun to take its toll subconsciously. The attacks themselves were not as terrifying for me as the aftermath. My brother Byron and I were commuting together in my car to our respective jobs in Bethesda, Maryland when the first plane hit. We were shocked to hear the radio station interrupt its programming to announce a plane hit the one of the Twin Towers in New York City. Our conversation continued after the news without reference to it. Then the newscaster announced a second plane struck the other tower at the World Trade Center a few minutes later.

We wondered together what was occurring. I dropped Byron off at National Institutes of Health where he worked in human resources and drove across Wisconsin Avenue to my client site on the campus of the National Naval Medical Center (now Walter Reed). As soon as I got situated at my desk, news arrived that a plane struck the Pentagon. I called Byron and we arranged to meet outside to get out of dodge with the exchange of only a few words. The uncertainty about the scope of the attacks led us to depart our government compounds in an affluent suburb. Nobody was attacking the least valued areas with the least-valued people in America (except its inhabitants). It felt like the world was standing still around us as very few cars were on the road. There was ominous silence at the gas station when we stopped to fill up.

By the time the impact of the day's devastation was known fully, Byron and I were back in the 'hood in the manner of the character Shine in Black folklore. (He was a laborer on the Titanic who had swum to Harlem by the time news of the invincible ship's sinking got around the world). Not until I heard a psychologist on television discussing the effects of post-traumatic stress on the nation's collective psyche several months later, did I realize I had been traumatized by the church. Another five years passed before I received treatment for it while in therapy for something unrelated.

This was the first time I was not either employed or in school full-time in almost 30 years. I was relieved as this was the rest my soul needed. Even a two-week vacation remains foreign to me to this day. The downtime allowed me to decompress from the stress of pursuing ordained ministry as well as the angst of failing to do so over the previous five years. My similarly-situated friends and I hung at each other's homes at all times of the day like we were in college again. My new neighbors suspected I was a drug dealer due to the heavy traffic and frequent deliveries. Imagine their relief when I told them I was a kept woman.

Increasing my time in communion with God was a priority. The rapid pace of life was quite a departure from the spiritual immersion my seminary experience provided. I returned to my lecture notes and began reading books I did not have the opportunity to explore in school. It was time to get ready for whatever was next.

Some churches act like you have to get a Top-Secret security clearance to have the privilege of serving in ministry, although the quality of what comes from their pulpits and classrooms does not reflect due diligence. Positions are assigned using superfluous criteria while so much talent goes to waste. Rev. Matthews did not concern himself with examining me further and appointed me to two church committees. He also personally rounded up established church leaders for a Bible study I would lead. It put wind beneath my wing and helped me realize that nothing on earth can thwart what God has purposed. He has been my greatest advocate to this day.

The class was a yearlong survey of the entire canon using denominational resources. Half of the students were old enough to be my parents, but remained very receptive to my leadership. One of the associate pastors approached me after we were well underway advising that I was not supposed to be teaching the Bible, but simply presenting the material provided. I responded, "a trained monkey can play a video and turn pages in a book. If I am going to spend my time doing this, I will leverage my expertise." Not one member of the class objected and neither did the pastor. The next scheduled class was a year-long survey of Christian theology. I declined to lead it because there was absolutely no chance the proceedings would not bear my imprint.

During the first Sunday sermon I delivered at Asbury, none other than Evans Crawford, Dean Emeritus of Rankin Chapel, was front and center. Never have I been more intimidated. He was a member of the congregation, but kept a low profile in retirement. Every word from his mouth seemed directly from above even in conversation. He marveled that he had never heard my text exegeted in the manner I had. His lavish praise was inspiring. The fact that Rev. Matthews trusted me with the pulpit in his absence moved me. It also felt good to express flattering remarks about a pastor without fear of being struck by lightning.

As I continued to regain my footing in faith, God beckoned me to visit the Grand Canyon. I was first inspired to do so immediately after my initial sermon, but never followed through. A business trip took me to Phoenix in November of 2003. I arrived a few days early with great anticipation of making my ascent to the edge of that big hole in the ground. One of my best friends from freshman year in college lived in a suburb of Phoenix. He was likewise looking forward to my visit as we had not seen each other in quite some time. As I deplaned and approached the rental car area, God told me to go straight to the Grand Canyon. I drove north from the airport under clear sunny skies and warm dry Arizona air without a second thought.

My friend, Demetrius, called me an hour or so after my plane landed to inquire about my whereabouts. He was alarmed to hear I was making the trip alone and in the evening.

"Are you crazy?" he shouted in a manner uncharacteristic of his easygoing personality.

"You already know the answer to that question."

"Turn around. It's dangerous."

I responded, "God said go and I'm going."

"There are elk on the road that will wipe you out if you hit one. It's not like hitting a deer. They are huge!"

A calm took over our conversation and I continued onward not knowing what laid ahead in my journey. Within an hour, night began to fall as I ascended to the rim of the canyon. Eventually, it became so dark I had to flicker the vehicle's headlights to ensure they were activated. No homes, businesses, or streetlights were on the side of the road from which to glean light. The temperature also fell steadily with the increase in elevation. I was in too deep to turn around and simply relied on God's guidance for illumination. In the final hour, there were not even any other vehicles on the road. It was pitch black with stars twinkling in the sky just enough to let me know they were there. I arrived at the Grand Canyon's Historic Village and could finally see in front of me, but not the destination itself. And it was freezing.

The next day, I arose at daybreak like Moses going to meet God face-to-face on the mountain. I prayed, ate breakfast, and walked to the Visitor's Center. Words cannot express my surprise to arrive at the South Rim, look down, and not see the Grand Canyon. I was standing above the clouds. A park ranger explained that a rare phenomenon called a cloud inversion was occurring. This happens when the air near the ground is colder than the air above it, causing any moisture between them to form a sea of clouds that fills the cavity. I walked around the rim in one direction for about an hour, returned to my original point and then walked in the other direction like my position would change its visibility.

Of all days for this to happen! Had I waited until later in the day to drive from warm, sunny Phoenix to Flagstaff, I would have seen the natural wonder clearly. But this was the appointed time God led me to visit the canyon. Why was God concealing what God clearly called me to experience? Then the stark similarity to my veiled faith journey hit me. I could not stop laughing. Just because I could not see the Grand Canyon did not by any means imply it was not there. Nor did it negate the existence of the divine.

The clouds were dense, bright, white, and billowing. They extended for miles in each direction. I had to take the majesty of nature that was given to me over the one I anticipated. I did not feel the need to stay up there all day to wait for the clouds to disappear and therefore left. Clouds appeared to me as a sign of divine presence just as they did to others so many times in Scripture. The trip back to Phoenix revealed treacherous twists and turns in the winding rocky road that I could have never navigated safely the night before without God's direction.

The following July, I enjoyed an aerial view of the full length of the 277-mile-long canyon during the return flight from my sorority's 47th National Convention in Las Vegas. It was far more spectacular than I could have ever experienced on the ground. The early morning sun made the red rocks appear to be ablaze. I peered through the window simply awestruck as I had no idea such a sight was on the flightpath. In that moment, God reminded me to persevere in faith with transcendence. For the Word says in that great day, my faith shall become sight.

What happened immediately following my trip simply blew my mind. Some of the members of Asbury had grown restless. They wanted a leader with more flash and pizzazz. Never mind the fact that Rev. Matthews was an excellent administrator and broke the bread fresh with expert precision. With a stroke of the bishop's pen, he was reassigned and a Replacement appointed to start in the summer of 2004. The Replacement did not know me personally, but there was tension between us from the beginning. Turns out, he was once a minister in the AME Church and knew my previous Presiding Elder.

I kept an open mind, but the joker looked strangely familiar. The quality of teaching, preaching, and management declined immediately. Then I remembered: *Beloved, do not believe every spirit, but test the spirits to see whether they are from God, because many false prophets have gone out into the world.*

Meanwhile, the congregation went wild in response to his theatrical antics in the pulpit in spite of his words having no redeeming value. "Did you see how he jumped around shouting today? He was on fire!" could be overheard after Sunday services. Never did I hear how the anointing on the message (or lack thereof) impacted their lives. Not only that, I never—in over a decade—heard him testify to a call or provide a single account of how God's spirit manifest in his life personally. Recounting second-hand testimonies is not credible witness.

Charge conference was held November of that same year. Rev. Matthews entered my name for ordination before he left and I was to be presented to the District Superintendent—the pastor's supervisor in the United Methodist Church—to advance my candidacy for ministry. When that time came on the agenda, The Replacement merely stated my name without even a mention of my education, experience, or a lukewarm endorsement. This was in contrast to another candidate who he presented at the same meeting. The Replacement gushed over him although I had been with the congregation longer and was more involved. I became disenchanted by the handwriting on the wall about how systemic my oppression was and stopped attending Asbury on a regular basis.

I dropped in from time to time over the next few years to check in with my fellow parishioners and show off my new wardrobe acquisitions. Eventually, I resolved to be more receptive of The Replacement's ministry. This was not the result in a change of heart, but rather justification for maintaining my social ties at the church. His preaching had not improved, so I brought homework to do during his sermons.

The year could not even get off to a good start before The Replacement stated one of the most ill-informed suppositions I have ever heard from a pulpit. Following one of the deadliest Israeli attacks on Gaza in January 2009, he said "Israel can kill all of the Arabs they want to secure the land because it is holy." More than 50 lives were lost in a bombing that included UN schools being used to house refugee families. His statement vexed my spirit. As people of the gospel, Christ has freed us from fighting carnally for God's sake and called us to otherworldliness.

Regardless of our political position, the war in Palestine is not ours to fight theologically. God's kingdom is not of this world. The Bible makes it quite obvious Jesus came not as a militaristic Messiah, but to provide a new life to believers by his Spirit. For that reason, his own received him not. Having this statement come during the morning's proclamation was no short of reckless. Washington, DC has a problem with violent crime, as does this nation overall. Imagine a misguided individual hearing justification for murder from the powerful position of the pulpit.

So many times while listening to preachers have I wanted God to state audibly, "That mess did not come from Me." This was one of them.

The crowd said "amen" on cue. I turned around in the middle of his message and asked "Did you hear what he just said?"

The man behind me said "No."

"Well, you said 'amen.'"

He responded, "It's just a habit."

For the first time in my life, I walked out of service in the middle of a sermon.

I went to the Bishop in Residence (a member of the episcopacy who is assigned to a local church or seminary, usually after retirement) at the conclusion of service. He confirmed the message was pure ignorance. A professor of religion at a local seminary was also a member of the congregation. He agreed with our position. Trying to give him the benefit of the doubt, I went to The Replacement's office immediately to discuss the theological implications of what he stated. Maybe I heard him wrong. Maybe his words got twisted. Maybe he needed to go.

After the last person left his office, I approached him calmly and laid out my case. He did not take issue with the points I raised. Rather, he was more offended that a young woman with no standing in the denomination dared to address him with such audacity. I broke out my Bible and went point-by-point through the inconsistency of his message not only with the gospel of Christ—which he acted like he was hearing for the first time—but also with the denomination's position.

The United Methodist Church has a clear policy on Palestine, which pushes for reconciliation. The Book of Social Principles describes Arab-Palestinians as oppressed people needing justice and relief. He stared at me with that "who the hell do you think you are" look I know so well. I wrote the conference's bishop to express my concern about the weak pulpit and spiritual decline of the congregation. He responded telling me basically to kiss his hind parts.

Out of deference to The Replacement's position, I sojourned for a year to the church in Baltimore where one of my linesisters was in ministry to mitigate further conflict. Upon my return, I joined a weekly Bible study group and attempted to start one several times. The pastor approved, but God held me back. My motivation was more so to position myself for a third attempt at ordination than to fulfill God's will for my life. Sometime after my return, the Replacement preached a sermon retracting the one that outraged me.

"That's as close to an apology as you are going to get" the Bishop in Residence said as he approached me at the conclusion of the service.

I shrugged and replied, "Honestly, I never expected one."

It is a wonder how God takes us to heights spiritually only to drop us back in the valley. Why can we not build tents on the mountain tops and let the mere mortals fend for themselves? Then God revealed to me that God did not call me to sit under someone's spiritual teat for the rest of my life. The change in altitude was part of the divine plan. *There is a time for everything and a season for every activity under the heavens.* And it was time for me to leave.

That's where the madness jumps off. Just as members of the military swear to defend this country against all enemies, foreign and domestic, disciples must battle God's enemies from within and beyond. That does not make me too many friends in the church. The institution's worldliness not only suits counterfeit preachers, but also provides comfort to spiritual slackers. Jesus warned his disciples. *If the world hates you, keep in mind that it hated me first. If you belonged to the world, it would love you as its own. As it is, you do not belong to the world, but I have chosen you out of the world. That is why the world hates you.*

Churchgoing can become a bad habit. We must rid God's house of darkness so it can bear light to the world as it should. It will not be easy because a lot is at stake on both sides. The enemy is always seeking whom he may devour especially those who are called according to God's purpose. Institutionalized religion is more concerned with good metrics and public relations. Each believer must decide for themselves how fruitful their participation is. It is hard to gauge. Therefore, we must enlist accountability partners within and beyond our immediate circles for more objectivity. Hell will be bursting at the seams with people with impressive church credentials. I broke the habit so I would not be one of them.

George Washington had been focusing on multiple business interests before accepting the inevitable nomination to be Commander in Chief during the American Revolution. He said, "You may believe me...when

I assure you, in the most solemn manner, that, so far from seeking this appointment I have used every endeavor in my power to avoid it."[7] In that same spirit have I approached ministry since completing my theological studies.

I returned to my pre-seminary occupation as a management consultant and volunteered with many noble causes to occupy my leisure time. None of my jobs were fulfilling and it showed in my performance. I simply could not throw myself into my work like I could before seminary.

The adage "no good deed goes unpunished" rang true in my altruism. I worked on political campaigns, volunteered at a suicide hotline, tutored in afterschool programs, advocated for and supported DC's public library system, served on non-profit boards, and even held elected office. My benevolence became burdensome as I dealt with ingratitude, disrespect, betrayal, racism, and at times, downright boredom. Each experience left me with no incentive to continue the ruse.

The first thing I did upon returning to DC after graduating from seminary was to sign up for Vice President Al Gore's presidential campaign. I am not a staunch Democrat, but felt a kindred spirit with him as a nerd's nerd. We share a passion for public service and both go deeper than most people to explore an issue. Gore also had a brief stint in seminary prior to entering politics. A Duke classmate who was an appointee in in the Clinton administration got me access to opportunities to be a surrogate speaker, health policy advisor, and outreach coordinator through the Democratic National Committee's headquarters. It was fulfilling to meet likeminded people and connect with old acquaintances.

On November 7, 2000, I went to sleep after newscasters claimed victory for Gore in Florida, pushing him over the necessary electoral college threshold for the presidency. All the hours I put into the campaign positioned me well for a job in the new administration. My heart sank when I awoke to the subsequent balloting discrepancies that reversed the outcome. Some who worked alongside me went to Florida to oversee the recounts. I had not yet accumulated enough leave on my day job, but remained in the struggle locally during off-hours. When the Supreme Court handed down its decision ending the recounts on December 12, I was protesting on Massachusetts Avenue outside the

Vice President's house. The harrowing news from passing motorists made me feel like there was no justice in the world.

My library advocacy was the most striking disappointment. What could be more safe and apolitical? Supporters of public libraries are the quintessential affluent, blue-haired old lady crowd. The DC Board of Library Trustees approved the construction of a new $15M edifice designed by world-renowned architect David Adjaye around the corner from my house. The existing library branch was a non-descript, utilitarian, World War II era building. I was excited at the prospect of living near something aesthetically pleasing.

Bellevue, the neighborhood where I bought my house, is quiet and stable, but quite unlivable according to planning indices. It dates back to the late 1800s and is one of the southernmost areas of the city. The neighborhood was once farmland, but developed residentially in the 1950s and 1960s. The original population was predominantly white. That changed following the Brown v. Board of Education Supreme Court decision desegregating schools and the resulting white flight. Many of my neighbors are empty nesters who are aging in place. My house and those immediately around it are nice, but the surrounding areas are underdeveloped blight.

Community leaders in my section of the city opposed the construction of a new library out of fear of gentrification. I spent four years as President of the library's Friends organization advancing the cause, volunteering in multiple capacities at the branch, developing programming, and monitoring the construction project. The organization's entire operational budget came straight from my pocket. I was elected Advisory Neighborhood Commissioner (a relatively powerless position halfway between Councilmember and dogcatcher) to eliminate opposition to the library by my predecessor. The groundbreaking was very emotional. The project manager presented me with a hard hat and neon vest to welcome me to visit the construction site at any time. I took pictures of the progress during my frequent visits from beginning to end. The library was my baby and these were my sonogram images.

My friends who lived in other places kept asking incredulously, "Who in the world opposes a new library?" Ward 8 has a 67% functional illiteracy rate. The last thing its residents should have been fighting was a library. It was surreal. I spent an inordinate amount of time appealing to city leaders, testifying before the City Council, presenting to the Zoning Board, mobilizing the community, planning new programs, and doing whatever else was necessary to make this possibility a reality. Adrian Fenty, the mayor at the time, pushed aggressively to fund new schools and libraries, but did not advocate actively for our branch as did no other leader from our community. National consumer advocate Ralph Nader paid some ragtag mercenary activists to oppose the construction. The Trustees, Council, and Zoning board eventually approved the redeveloped library for the Bellevue neighborhood.

There is a saying that "failure is an orphan, but success has many parents." Just when things seemed to be progressing smoothly with the library, William Lockridge, the School Board representative for my area, passed away suddenly in January 2011—three years into the development process. Mayor Vincent Gray, who had just taken office at the beginning of the year, proposed naming something prominent after him while paying tribute at his funeral. As I was exiting the service, a neighbor whispered in my ear that they were coming after the library. I developed a splitting headache in an instant that lasted for weeks. This move was without consultation with the Board of Library Trustees, Federation of Friends of DC Public Library, the branch's Friends organization, immediate community, or anyone else with some skin in the game. The building's namesake's only connections to the branch were being expelled from the previous building for drunken and disorderly conduct and opposing its construction on the record. I was undone.

My City Council representative happened to be none other than DC's former mayor, Marion Barry. He watched the contentious debate over the library's construction from the sidelines. He silently supported it, but did not want to openly counter his allies who were all on the other side. Barry summonsed me one evening the following month to meet him at the Players' Lounge, a dive bar where he was known to hold court. I only ordered a Diet Coke. Barry acknowledged my staunch advocacy and said if I continued to advance the new library, he would stay out of the way of the naming debate. The Chair of the Board of Library Trustees, who was also the CEO of the very influential Federal City Council, held a backdoor meeting with Mayor Gray the following month. They agreed to kill the proposed legislation soon after its introduction to the City Council.

The Board of Library Trustees voted that summer to change the name to Bellevue to reflect the far Southwest neighborhood where it is actually located. Ironically, the branch had been named Washington Highlands for its first fifty years after a nearby neighborhood. The mayor reintroduced the long-stalled bill at the beginning of the next legislative session after Lockridge's widow, Wanda, got wind of the Trustees' move. During the Council hearings, the mayor allowed reason to prevail and surprisingly withdrew his recommendation. He suggested honoring the decedent another way. His supporters ironically did not want to put his name on any of the failing schools he represented.

I could not get too happy as DC Public Library leaders left me hanging by not showing up as the government's witness at the September 2011 City Council hearing before the Committee of the Whole to present its extensive testimony in opposition. They opted to submit it in writing for the record instead of even having a staffer read it. I have never seen such before or since. The children of several Barry cronies also suddenly got jobs eight months into Vincent Gray's administration all the way up to his Deputy Chief of Staff. The only bargaining chip I had with Marion Barry was my body, but it was not in play. Library staff members told me they suspected their leadership betrayed me and cut a deal with the mayor. Gray spent a lot of political capital and effort on such a minor issue to get DCPL to relent. That is not to mention how he flouted established laws and governance structures defining how the library naming process occurs.

Wanda Lockridge marched defiantly upstairs to the mayor's office immediately after the hearing. His staff gave her a letter retracting his testimony from just one-hour prior. The Council followed the mayor blindly, eventually approving his request two months later. Ironically, the Council had not entangled itself in the affairs of the library system against elimination of Sunday hours, three consecutive years of budget cuts, or to ensure branches had adequate resources to meet the needs of their consumers. I have not entered the new library's doors since its opening feeling like the mother who lost her baby in the case before King Solomon. A neighbor described how gut-wrenching hearing its name unexpectedly during the ribbon cutting was. This level of disrespect would not have happened elsewhere in DC.

Vincent Gray left us with a city where you could not even volunteer at the library without encountering his filth. His administration was marked by scandal after scandal from beginning to end. I lost sleep, time off work, and money fighting as a veritable one-woman army. Not even Mr. Lockridge offered any support when asked directly, nor did he participate in library programming when requested. Gray rubbed my face in his ability to commandeer the issue. That stung because I was once a fan and signed up for his campaign the day after he announced.

The fruit of my labor became a monument to low expectations and public corruption. The Bellevue neighborhood has the dubious distinction of having the only branch in the city whose name does not meet DC Public Library's official standards. Two branches bear the names of Civil Rights luminaries Martin Luther King and Dorothy Height. Two others are named for the late Chair of the Board of Library Trustees, Francis A. Gregory, and Juanita E. Thornton, a retired DC school teacher and community activist who led the campaign to develop a new branch in the Shepherd Park neighborhood. Ours is marred by the name of a man of no prominence, scholarship, or library-related advocacy as required by DC Public Library policy.

No public record exists of the rationale for Mayor Gray's reversal. However, I volunteered on his campaign as did the decedent and his wife. She acted like she did not even know him during campaign meetings which he attended with another woman in tow, but placed a full-sized box of tissues on the table for her crocodile tears at the Council hearing. What the mayor did not know is I kept receipts in the form of typewritten, date-stamped meeting minutes. He also did not know the man he was seeking to honor came to several campaign meetings staggeringly drunk and disruptive.

The mayor did not know these things because he kept his distance from field operations that were later revealed to be financed by over $600,000 in illegal campaign contributions from a one of the city's largest healthcare contractors. We met regularly in a storefront office space walking distance from Gray's house. I am also not sure whether

Gray knew the decedent absconded with a large sum of that ill-gotten cash he was supposed to use to pay for buses and out-of-state workers on election day. A flurry of calls went out to other campaign workers to collect enough money to cover the expenses. I received one of those calls.

Among my notes were large-scale activities not documented in the mayor's official campaign reports. It appeared to me that the mayor was being blackmailed by Lockridge's widow. I shared my notes with federal prosecutors when they interviewed me about the shadow campaign. The allegations never saw daylight because Vincent Gray was never formally indicted. However, they had some degree of merit as the city's Chief Librarian resigned and relocated to the west coast without explanation soon after being questioned by the FBI about the subsequent restoration of $7.5M previously cut from the library's operating budget and a new allocation to its capital budget of over $100M to renovate the city's central library. The President of the Board of Library Trustees accepted the CFO position for the city of Detroit around the same time. No one was as happy as me when karma remembered Vince Gray's address in 2014 when he suffered a humiliating defeat in his bid for re-election.

A Barry confidante called me at home toward the end of the legislative review cycle.

"What are you willing to do to get the Councilmember to support your position?"

"What do you mean?" I replied.

There was a pregnant pause. I furrowed my brow and added "I ain't sucking nothing!"

He hung up abruptly without saying another word. Barry called me early one morning about a week later to negotiate further. I told him I had no respect for him for betraying me and had nothing further to say. A voice sounding like Wanda Lockridge's asked softly in the background "Why are you calling her now?" I cannot say what she did or did not do to get her way. But I do recall a good friend's mom telling me when I was younger that success was not sucking anything you do not want to suck. Like in the church, I came up short again by remaining too principled for my environment.

Following Barry's passing in November 2014, every aspiring politician in Ward 8 declared their candidacy for his vacant City Council seat—including me. I was reluctant initially because private life is far more energizing. While serving in various civic capacities, I was always at some meeting or another. If not, my phone rang incessantly with someone making a request or simply wanting to wax politically.

The pressure to run was more external than internal. Neighbors, fellow public servants, and friends encouraged me. My mother thought I had lost my mind. She was right. Being in the public eye constantly in such a high-maintenance area does not suit my introverted and contemplative nature. After ten days of collecting signatures and appealing to residents, I withdrew. The official reason was to spend more time with my dog. The real reason was to return my focus to my unfinished business with God.

5

TRAUMA DRAMA

In love's service, only wounded soldiers can serve.

Thornton Wilder

Psychological trauma is defined as an emotionally shocking experience which has a lasting psychic effect, usually categorized as post-traumatic stress disorder.[8] "Trauma is not only a deeply disturbing and immobilizing experience. It is also subjective. (W)hat matters most are the individual's internal beliefs and their innate sensitivity to stress, not whether a family member, therapist or other outsider deems an experience traumatic."[9] A person is the judge and jury of whether or not they have been injured psychologically. More often than not, people do not have a name or language to affix to the effects of their experience.

Trauma has a wide variety of causes, but some common characteristics. There is frequently a violation of the person's core assumptions about the world and their human rights, putting the person in a state of extreme confusion and insecurity. This is seen when institutions depended upon for survival violate, humiliate, betray, or cause major losses or separations instead of evoking aspects like positive self-worth, safe boundaries and personal freedom.[10] Betrayal trauma occurs when the people or institutions on which a person depends for survival significantly violate that person's trust or well-being.[11] "Traumatic events are extraordinary, not because they occur rarely, but rather because they overwhelm the ordinary human adaptations to life."[12]

My most significant trauma resulted from the shock of learning the church was not the safe place I assumed. My parents are quite protective. They still want to know my whereabouts well into middle age and expect me to check in periodically to assure them of my well-being. Their sending me to Sunday School every week throughout my childhood was quite an endorsement. As I grew in faith, I continued attending church into adulthood without any sense of guardedness. That is until the slow-moving collision between my assumptions and the reality I faced as I pursued ordained ministry.

Picture this: RFK Stadium, Washington, DC, November 18, 1985. It was the break heard around the world. The ball was on the home team's 46-yard line. The snap was routine. The quarterback received the ball and searched for the optimal receiver. Seemingly, out of nowhere, Lawrence Taylor, a defensive end from the opposing New York Giants and the best in the league at the time, tackled Joe Theismann. The quarterback's two lower right leg bones broke midway between his knees.

Millions of viewers witnessed the injury. They could not believe their eyes even though there was no mistaking what occurred. In case there was any doubt, the broadcasters replayed the scene what felt like dozens of times that evening alone from every angle imaginable. Then newscasters and other television programs around the country aired the footage repeatedly for days to come. Regardless of whether or not one was a football fan at the time, viewing that gruesome scene became inevitable.

There was no mistaking that Joe Theismann's career was over. He was a hero who distinguished himself on and off the field. People admired him nationwide even if they were not fans of Washington's football team. The level of empathy was like nothing I have ever seen—even to this day.

Being a native Washingtonian, I lived through this drama in what felt like an intimate way. My father is a diehard fan of the local football franchise and takes every triumph and defeat personally. He is over the moon when they win. We cannot speak to him when they lose. When the team loses to their rival Dallas Cowboys (my preferred team), he must be left alone all together.

The local news showed the footage of Joe Theismann's injury daily for over a year. Viewers received updates on his treatment, therapy, prognosis, and every move for many months to come. I can imagine that his medical team knew immediately what was wrong. Physicians were on the sidelines. They viewed the injury firsthand and had immediate access to the video footage.

Radiologists confirmed the diagnosis by executing the necessary imaging, laying the groundwork for a treatment plan. Orthopedists performed surgery to reposition the bones and insert the plates and screws needed to hold everything in place until the fracture healed. Physical therapists worked with him to improve how his leg could bear his weight and prepare him to begin walking in subsequent weeks. There was widespread optimism that he would recover and get on with his life with the best medical team at his disposal.

The end of the Joe Theismann era followed the stages of grief as if a loved one had died. Nevertheless, he moved on and created a career as a businessman and sports commentator. The outpouring of sympathy for him over the way his career was disrupted opened doors far wider than if his career-ending injury had never occurred.

Not to this day—over 30 years later—have I heard one person dare suggest he should have returned to the game after mending his wounds. Whatever he decided, or was decided for him by the circumstances, was accepted without questioning.

Joe Theismann admits to viewing the clip only one time and "that the moment remains fresh for him, even as it enters its fourth decade." Local news organizations still run commemorative stories about it during each milestone anniversary.

Likewise, I was severely injured, but nobody was the wiser. Not even me.

The first blow came at the end of my first year of seminary. My childhood friend Neptina had been diagnosed with colon cancer at the age of twenty-six around the same time I discerned my call to ministry. It seemed so farfetched. She was a decorated police officer and an athletic physical specimen. Even her doctors did not take her complaints seriously initially. They told her Black women her age did not come to them with colon cancer. But she insisted on pursuing multiple opinions.

Neptina and I went way back. She was that straight, no chaser friend everyone needs. We first met when she moved to my neighborhood from a tough area of Northwest DC and transferred to my elementary school. During her first week, she got into a fight with a classmate. The classmate's older sister came from the nearby junior high after school to confront her. Neptina proceeded to beat her up too. I knew right then and there that we would be tight.

We cut up together in Sunday School. (Her parents caught on to the free childcare hustle with a quickness). We both played clarinet in the DC Youth Orchestra. We worked summer jobs together. We assembled our wardrobes together in the stores of downtown DC as we came into our own in high school. We shared bad luck in romantic relationships. We pursued our respective careers with intensity. We even attained milestones in faith around the same time.

Neptina and I drifted apart while I was in college and graduate school, but always picked up where we left off whenever we reconnected. I was honored that she shared not only her diagnosis, but also her spiritual angst, with me. God grew me up with this sacred trust. Most days, all I could do was sit in stunned silence at what she conveyed. I had few answers for her, but lots of love. My greatest lesson was that this was not a problem to be solved, but rather an experience to be shared.

Most disturbing was how some religious people told her that her illness was due to a lack of faith. That angered me to no end, but I thought on some level we could pray it away. We cannot pray our way out of the human condition. Realizing chemotherapy was only postponing the inevitable, Neptina ceased treatment and stared death in the face without one bit of fear. Her last words to me were that nothing in this life was worth clinging to and she was ready to be with God. Colon cancer took Neptina out of this world the day before her thirtieth birthday. I never imagined our friendship would not extend into our golden years.

The pain of separation by death of a loved one can be profound. Psychologists place the natural limit for the number of people the human brain can connect with deeply enough that their death would leave one devastated at between ten and fifteen.[13] Neptina was one of mine unbeknownst to me. Her death was so earth-shattering that I collapsed to the floor upon hearing the news and I could not compose myself to pay tribute during her funeral. Even her pastor cried throughout the eulogy in one of the most humane acts of ministry I have ever witnessed. It was tragic. Her passing made no sense. Surely, God has some other people in mind without whom the world would be better. I could name names if necessary.

Contrast this with the ridiculous trend in negating mourners' grief by forcing them to celebrate the passing of a loved one while the pain is still fresh. The most powerful emotional moment of our Lord and Savior's earthly life is captured in the shortest verse of the Bible. *Jesus wept.* Upon learning of his friend Lazarus' death, Jesus did not rejoice because his friend was in a better place. He did not tell Lazarus' sisters how to feel. He did not try to prove he was impervious to the range of human emotions. He cried. And he did not just shed a tear. He lost control, got ugly in the face, and sobbed from the depths of his soul. Modern narcissistic preachers would have responded differently. "Y'all shut up! I'm about to bring him back from the dead."

The first biblical account of a proper burial is recorded in Genesis 23:19. Throughout Scripture, we find individuals and communities grieving losses and performing rites befitting the occasions. Even the Law of Torah establishes protocols for handling corpses. Death is a sacred event so it is only fitting that the funeral be a solemn occasion to honor not only the dearly departed, but also their loved ones' journey from sorrow to joy. I want lots of flowers, black attire, and crying at my funeral. It would be nice if someone tries to jump in the grave as my body is being interred yelling, "Take me with you!"

There is no shame in observing traditional rites for the deceased. My family sat through my uncle's funeral while the preacher admonished his children and siblings not to grieve. "This is a celebration!" he repeated several times throughout the service with the casket front and center. That was easy for him to say as it was not his loved one. Such toxic positivity amounts to professional malpractice.

And please stop referring to funerals as homecomings. I kid you not, I have seen the Freudian slip of the intended "homegoing" moniker used more than once because people are in a mindset far from respectful mourning. If you find yourself delighting in someone else's loved one's passing, do them a favor and keep it to yourself. We must be mindful to be sensitive on occasions such as these. Scripture implores us to *rejoice with those who rejoice and weep with those who weep.* It does not tell us to cheer up those in the throes of grief. Rather we are told *Blessed are those who mourn, for they will be comforted.* Walking on holy ground requires one to remove one's shoes and tread carefully. Grieving is a complex process warranting mindful consideration.

Jean Paul Sartre was accurate in his description of Christianity as a breeder of psychosis, the mental disorder characterized by gross detachment from reality and the inability to function in it. He described the dynamic as "bad faith" when people lie to themselves for the sake of expediency. "[Bad faith] is a certain art of forming contradictory ideas which unite in themselves the negation of that idea."[14] Religious sensibilities dictate that we act ecstatic while sinking into despair, feign enlightenment when confounded by life's challenges, and shout "amen" at nonsense while our spiritual needs go unmet. All the while, adherents of bad faith deny their freedom to choose otherwise.

Grieving Neptina came on top of things not going well in my own world. She lived right and seemingly had her whole life ahead of her. The foundation was laid. She walked upright, took care of herself, honored her parents, and was pursuing a bachelor's degree part-time in the midst of a flourishing career in law enforcement. My girl purchased a condominium in her early twenties that was laid out well enough to be featured in a shelter magazine. She never married nor had children. Why did God allow this? What was in store for me?

The second blow landed the spring of my second year of seminary. That was the time when the church would have ordained me had events unfolded normally. I tried in vain to work around Rev. Nobody with the standing to do so would advocate for me. I reached out to my professor who offered to intervene previously. She responded that she could do nothing for me. From that moment forward, she became as salty as Lot's wife toward me. Challenging the status quo required escalation. I wrote the conference bishop, (henceforth known at The Right Reverend), who was also the Presiding Elder's supervisor. He left a voicemail at my parents' house in DC, but never returned my calls or attempted to contact me in Atlanta. In addition to avoiding me like the plague, the bishop never provided a written response to my letter.

The Washington Annual Conference convened toward the end of April, just as my semester was concluding, under the direction of The Right Reverend. Nobody from Allen Chapel contacted me to request my presence or inform me of any change of status. I ran to my apartment between classes to wait by the phone in case the bishop tried to reach me to make things right. I pushed myself academically as if torture would please God enough to force the bishop's hand. The phone never rang.

Greek II and a doctoral-level seminar on Danish theologian Søren Kierkegaard were among my electives. Most days, I did nothing other than walk my dog and put my nose to the grindstone—no socializing, no recreational activities, no television. The phone never rang. Rev.'s initial warmth toward me provided a glimmer of hope that he would eventually concede. But the fact remained that I never relented to his illicit demands and he had a reputation to uphold. I was crestfallen at the end of the day of the ordination service and cried my eyes out with no one to hear. A seasoned minister in the denomination told me I sealed my fate the moment I wrote the bishop.

Studying Kierkegaard at that time was my saving grace. His writings spoke to me so poignantly that I walked the halls with my nose in his writings between classes and immersed myself in his canon at home. Few understood why I was so flipped out by "The Dane," as he is known affectionately by his devotees. His mingling of Christian theology with existential philosophy forced me to begin to find my true self apart from my social and religious origins. *Fear and Trembling* explores faith as a huge risk. Kierkegaard portrays faith as a paradox between resignation and engaging the absurd (e.g., nihilism v. playing the fool). It is best summarized by Job's testimony: *Though he slay me, yet will I trust in him.*

Works of Love illuminates what a life of faith is all about in concrete, rather than abstract, terms. Kierkegaard too struggled with "Christendom" because the institution he experienced was not the embodiment of Christ, i.e. the church, for him. As a matter of fact, he wrote an entire book titled *Attack Upon "Christendom"* against the established order of the church. He also failed to get ordained by human hands.

The mass shooting at Columbine High School occurred right before one of our weekly sessions. A young Jewish doctoral student burst into the room as we assembled demanding the instructor cancel class due to the tragedy. I sat there in shock that she requested such a thing. People I knew got shot frequently when I was growing up and our schools never skipped a beat. There was no way I was going to miss savoring the works that had become a salve to my soul, let alone waste the good money I was paying for the pleasure. She acted like I was some kind of monster for taking that position. The instructor allowed a moment of silence and proceeded with the day's agenda. Funny enough, the requestor remained and participated fully.

Almost on cue, my best-friend-in-my-head, Renita Weems, released her seminal book, *Listening for God: A Ministers Journey Through Silence and Doubt*, as my crisis peaked. I bought it immediately and devoured the pages in the midst of a demanding course load. Although she is a biblical scholar, accomplished writer, and renowned preacher, this work represented her own spiritual memoir and theological manifesto. Weems discussed how she triumphed in faith despite seasons when God appeared to hide God's face from her. I never could have imagined such an anointed and accomplished woman shared my struggles. Meeting her soon thereafter at a reading in Atlanta was a supreme pleasure. When I told her what I was experiencing with the AME Church and how edifying her writings were, she questioned why I was suffering willingly and advised me to leave.

No one else at that point recognized or affirmed my injury. So many spiritually wounded people walk around without notice or care. These injuries do not lend themselves to diagnostic imaging as with bone fractures or soft tissue ruptures. These wounds are inflicted by what is called "radical evil" in theological circles. Immanuel Kant coined the term to describe when people choose self-interest over moral law either individually or collectively. He contended that being evil is more a matter of the failure to exercise free choice of the good than an inherent disposition. In religious communities, it can manifest as keeping the peace as opposed to confronting wrong-doing. Members on the receiving end are especially vulnerable because they do not have their defenses activated to protect themselves in the way they would in the world.

Individuals can experience radical evil that immobilizes them spiritually. I hurt deeper in my being than imaginable. Many nights I groaned with existential anguish that defied clinical diagnosis. The default response of the church is first to blame the victim. I was told directly and indirectly that I must have done something to find myself on the receiving end of sexual harassment. Did I lead Rev. to think I was the type of woman he could pimp? Were my hemlines too short and necklines too revealing? Nobody who knew him denied he was a creep, but addressing that would have been too disruptive. People's lives are not collateral damage for members' comfort and the institutions' survival.

On top of that, members marginalize victims' experiences and beckon them to get back into the game prematurely. Taking time away from organized religion can be restorative. Not going to church after such a crippling spiritual injury was the most self-preserving thing I could have done for myself at the time. I received multiple offers of ordination in the AME Church before eventually leaving. Not one of the pastors was willing to confront the situation that obstructed me in the first place. They wanted me to enter the same process with the same players so they could feel good about being complicit with a corrupt system. I politely declined each one.

Confronting evil in the body is essential for minimizing its effects. The first time anyone took stock of the spiritual and psychological damage resulting from my ordeal was my first post-seminary pastor. Rev. Matthews acknowledged the presence of such destructive dynamics in the body and nursed me back to health spiritually. Allowing me to preach and teach almost immediately after joining the congregation was an essential part of affirming I was totally welcome and not just the fragments of my life that suited the organization.

I have witnessed and experienced church people relish other people's suffering. Some feel morally superior since the cosmic roll of the dice spared them. Have they never heard *[God] causes his sun to rise on the evil and the good, and sends rain on the righteous and the unrighteous?* Others savor the devastation they inflict. It becomes a symbol of power to be a force to be reckoned with. Rev. held me up as an example of what happens to anyone who defied him. He even went so far as to call me "disobedient" from the pulpit. No one in the congregation questioned what it was I did not obey. They simply followed his lead and turned on me.

One of the reasons I endured our fight for three years was because I wanted to believe right would prevail. It was soul crushing when it became clear I would never be ordained in the only denomination to which I had ever belonged at that point. The fact that no one went to bat for me compounded the damage.

I interrupted the instructor during a seminary evangelism class as he lambasted people who refuse to have anything to do with organized Christianity—another way the church gaslights people. In his eyes, the task of the believer is to convert others to their way of thinking and being in the world. My interjection that some people have a legitimate claim against the institutional church was met with a scorned scowl. Lots of people do not come to church because they do not have an encounter with God there. Rituals, liturgy, doctrinal statements, and polity can be as obfuscating as they can be illuminating of the divine. That is not to mention the nature of interactions with people within the organization. I described to him how I heard more from God in the silence of creation on the bike trail and experienced more love from my fellow cyclists than I did during Sunday services. Some things cannot be faked. The professor looked at me as if he had never given the proposition any consideration, although he could not refute it.

On another occasion, the same professor challenged the class to devise ways to save failing congregations as presented in case studies. I was the only person in the class who took the position that maybe they just needed to die. He tightened his jaw and squinted at me for my failure to play along. Jesus said, *Truly, truly I say to you, unless a grain of wheat falls into the earth and dies, it remains alone; but if it dies, it bears much fruit.* This verse applies equally to individuals as well as organizations. There is nothing worse than a dead church continuing to operate past its shelf life.

Over the years, I have heard of scandal after of scandal within organized religion. The most prophetic voices tend to come from outside the fold. When court filings finally revealed Eddie Long to be the molester that rumors had been conveying for decades, it was not a voice from a pulpit, but comedienne Cadillac Kimberly who broke it down. She quipped ever so elegantly, "God said *touch not my anointed; and do my prophet no harm.* He ain't said nothing about Eddie Long." Upon news of Eddie Long's death, Christendom was quite polite and demure.

The only high-profile critic was blogger Son of Baldwin. He went in on Long's legacy and the enablement by passive observers in an essay titled "Bishop Eddie Long Is Not the Only One Who's Dead." Never have I encountered a scandal on that level without threadbare red flags all over the wreckage. The price we pay for acknowledging them is the path to the cross. *For there is nothing hidden that will not be disclosed, and nothing concealed that will not be known or brought out into the open.* In other words, what is done in the dark will always come to light.

Being so devoted to the business of the institution at the expense of its integrity is what has led to the decline of mainline Protestant churches. Its secrets are well-known, but owning up to them is foreign to the culture. An old adage says "confession is good for the soul." As much as we must confess our individual sins, the body needs corporate confession of its shortcomings and deliberate transgressions if it is to overcome them. The typical defiance in the face of inarguable offenses usually reserved for criminal elements have no place in a community claiming to represent God's presence in the world.

Those who inflict spiritual wounds walk with impunity. Some are sadistic and take great pleasure in abusing their power. Others are ignorant of the pain they have inflicted or insensitive to the plight of the victims. Whatever the case, their behavior is sociopathic. Lawrence Taylor was devastated by inflicting Joe Theismann's debilitating injury and motioned to the sideline for immediate medical assistance. Church folks kick victims to the curb and leave them for dead. At least that has been my experience.

Institutional betrayal is as common in the church as it is the world. Every girl or woman exploited sexually by her pastor, every boy molested by a priest, every faithful steward neglected during their time of need, every congregation whose pastor misappropriated the organization's finances, and every member marginalized because of their lowly income or social status has been punched in their spiritual gut. That is not to mention those scarred by bad teaching or cultish behavior to which they were exposed in their respective communities of faith.

Fragility is a luxury not afforded to Blacks in general. Our ancestors were whipped brutally for even the slightest offense during their enslavement and lynched for sport during Jim Crow. That type of terrorism was to send a message to onlookers to stay in their defined place without regard for the consequent emotional damage. A classmate in my dorm died in an automobile accident during my first semester of college. Grief counselors subsequently stationed in the lobby for the next few days. The Resident Assistant encouraged us to speak to one if we felt the need. I replied that I did not even know the deceased and had only seen him in passing.

The residual psychological effects of devaluing mental health remain in the Black community. People I actually knew well died during my teen and young adult years. No one ever checked on my feelings. I came of age during the Crack Era in our Nation's Capital. Bodies were dropping like flies mostly as the result of wanton violence and associated externalities. I saw the police processing crime scenes frequently as I walked to school in the morning without missing a beat.

As a matter of fact, my high school principal would include who among our peers got shot in his morning announcements over the intercom, followed by "have a great day" and the first period bell. One morning, students in my homeroom stared out the window as police pulled a body from the creek behind the school. A classmate said, "I hope that's not my brother because he didn't come home last night." Unfortunately, it was her brother and she was not even dismissed for the day. My peers and I were conditioned to suck up our pain and get on with our lives while the rest of the world celebrated our resilience.

And so, I tried to move on following my great distress with the church. There were many well-meaning people who were aware of the spiritual and psychic pain I bore during that season. A few pastors of my acquaintance offered to help me game the system and get ordained through back door means. Neither they, nor I, realized my injuries prohibited me from being able to function effectively. The difference between Joe Theismann and me is that he went out at the top of his game, while I had not yet gotten started in mine. The heights to which I could have ascended in ministry had Rev. not kneecapped me haunted me for many years to come.

God has a way of humbling the proud. Joe Theismann recalled what a self-centered, arrogant jerk he was before his career-ending injury. In the same manner, I was ambitious, egotistical, and insensitive prior to my downfall. Since then, I have become quite accessible, empathetic, and generous. In other words, I became more like Jesus. Anything that results in assuming more of his divine nature is a blessing. It took me years of navel-gazing to realize that.

An epiphany came to me from the experience of water seeping into the basement of my house. The problem persisted despite the installation of a sump pump. Removing the sheetrock and insulation revealed major cracks in the walls through which water would pass when the surrounding ground became saturated. A structural engineer informed me that the safety of the entire building was compromised because bowing walls can force the entire house to crumble. Therefore, it became essential to incur major expense to seal the cracks and reinforce the walls to keep the house intact.

So it is with people. Spiritual and psychic trauma have serious implications for our entire being. I reached a point where I could not function while in graduate school at Duke. My psychiatrist asked me about any losses during routine questioning. He became speechless as I rattled the names of dozens of deceased friends. Typical cases for him included privileged students experiencing academic challenges, romantic disappointments, or parental divorce. Here I come from an area where few people on campus dare tread. He asked incredulously whether I actually knew those people personally or only knew of them. Upon learning that I had endured what pretty much amounted to growing up in a warzone, he advised that my unprocessed grief had become immobilizing.

That was no stretch. One night during a college break, a friend and I had to crawl to the car on our knees and elbows while bullets flew overhead as we left The East Side—a DC nightclub known for violence. We never spoke of the incident again for over thirty years. Psychiatrist Robert Lifton noted that "unresolved or incomplete mourning results in stasis and entrapment in the traumatic process."[15] The pressure of being in an intensely competitive and hostile environment triggered the effects. Likewise, I walked around seminary for three years on the verge of a breakdown because of how Rev. violated my trust while I was most vulnerable and no one intervened.

Following graduation, I was mad at the world, and the God who made it, for things not working out the way I thought they should. This outcome was despite my walking upright and remaining true to my calling. Very little in my life during the ensuing years met my expectations. My first post-seminary pastor was the one person who took my call seriously and took responsibility for helping me to pursue a career in ministry. Rev. Matthews did a great work in helping me to reinforce my psychic walls, but years of therapy were required to seal the cracks.

So many wounded souls are scattered on the battlefield of the Lord. To add insult to injury, their fellow soldiers turn a blind eye to their condition. Pleading for them to pull themselves together and press on is as cruel and absurd as it would be in a physical war. One of the first ethics of the military is to leave no soldier behind. If a [person]-down situation presents itself, the unit takes the body to where it can receive proper treatment or interment.

Regrettably, there are those who abuse and exploit vulnerable people who come to the place where they should be safest. I let my guard down and believed the best about the people with whom I practiced faith, as do so many. Jesus said: *And whoever receives one such child in My name receives Me; but whoever causes one of these little ones who believe in Me to stumble, it would be better for him to have a heavy millstone hung around his neck, and to be drowned in the depth of the sea.* I have waited a long time for justice, but have not seen it in this life. The next life is too long to wait.

6

STOP THE MADNESS

Do not be deceived. Bad company corrupts good character.

I Corinthians 15:33

Iwent through a phase early in my ministry during which I tried to calculate how to navigate deviance in the church unscathed. First came the longer hemlines. Those proportions were not a good look for me at only five foot one. Then I tried to avoid any tops that revealed the presence of breasts on my chest. Nothing short of a tent could conceal an ample bosom on a petite frame. Like a city on a hill, they cannot be hid. Tailored details were most flattering for my wardrobe. Anything else would have me looking like a pilgrim.

A senior member of the fashionista guild at Allen Chapel assuaged my concerns. "You were fly when God called you. There's no need to change." Two male teen charges in the youth ministry asked me to promise not to get on the fast track to becoming matronly. They had a point as weight-gain and declining appearances are common with young women who are deeply religious. I had to admit church time had encroached on gym time. The fact that I exercised regularly was my saving grace for enduring the stress.

According to strength training expert Mark Rippetoe:

> If your expectations are always those of someone content
> to live without physical challenge, then when it comes to
> mental, moral, or emotional challenge you fail to meet it

because you are out of practice. Meeting and overcoming obstacles are skills that can be honed as opposed to talents with which we are born.[16]

Hence, weak specimens make for weak disciples. It comes as no surprise that religious organizations prone to social control do not encourage physical fitness. Eugene Peterson's paraphrase of I Corinthians 9:27 restates Paul's admonition along the same lines.

> *I don't know about you, but I'm running hard for the finish line. I'm giving it everything I've got. No sloppy living for me! I'm staying alert and in top condition. I'm not going to get caught napping, telling everyone else all about it and then missing out myself.*[17]

Rippetoe states further:

> If you can treat personal tragedy like a heavy set of 20 squats, you'll do better than someone who has never met any challenge. Intentionally placing yourself in the position of having to complete a task when you don't know if you can is the single best way of preparing to be in that position unintentionally.[18]

I did not make this correlation contemporaneously with my most intense struggles, but must admit working out kept me from despairing or resorting to physical violence. As a matter of fact, I found great relief while imagining punching specific people while taking cardio-boxing classes. A long-distance bike ride has proven to be more enlightening than hours upon hours of church attendance.

My systematic theology professor, who was more than twenty-five years my senior, invited me on a group ride as I tried to cope with my stress. I had not ridden much at all while in seminary, but looked down my nose at him like I could hang with whatever he brought. On Thanksgiving morning of my second year, about a dozen cyclists—almost all of whom were older and more experienced than me—rode through the backroads of suburban Atlanta for fifty miles. I trailed the entire time crying and calling on Jesus. Meanwhile, my professor glided gracefully with his quintessential Jamaican breeziness. When asked why he did not tell me how far we were going in advance, he replied that he knew I would not have agreed armed with that information. There he goes acting just like God. However, pushing myself physically certainly strengthened my resolve to finish the Christian race.

The fare served from almost every church's kitchen is not conducive to a balanced diet. Although I must admit, it is almost invariably delicious. I began padding on pounds as my time spent within the church building increased. Every day after work presented a class, meeting, or another responsibility. Some changes were in order. Gym time got rescheduled to early mornings before work. I also began bringing fruit, yogurt, nuts, and other healthy options to consume when I knew I would be at church for extended periods.

That problem increased when I moved down South. People usually brought their most show-stopping, yet unhealthy, dishes to potlucks. The first time I had homemade sweet tea down there, I almost experienced hyperglycemia. Being gracious by at least partaking of a little was essential as observers might speculate that I thought I was too good for their food.

Some denominations require licensed preachers to wear a combination of black and white while they await ordination. For the first two years following my entry into the process, that is pretty much all I wore within and outside the church. It was pretty exciting to me as I was raised to believe wearing black was reserved for mature women. I never even owned a black dress until I was twenty-one and preparing for a sorority ritual. A high school classmate was considered scandalous for wearing a black gown to our senior prom. I cringe to this day every time I see a young girl dressed in black. Wearing black so frequently made me feel sophisticated like a fully-grown woman.

Part of the motivation for the restricted wardrobe is to project a modest image. Monks have their cassocks. Nuns have their habits. Licentiates have their black and white. The other is a defense mechanism to ward off unwanted suitors. Neither works. A lot of flash can be executed with a monochromatic palette.

Predators will step out of line regardless. As Kahlil Gibran said, "Forget not that modesty is for a shield against the eye of the unclean."[19] It took several years after leaving the AME Church for me to begin integrating colors back into my wardrobe. The conservative Washingtonian in me still feels like I am wilding out by choosing navy business attire over black. If I am wearing bright colors, you know I am feeling myself. People will make advances if you are wearing sackcloth and ashes if they are so inclined.

The rumor mill begins to churn as soon as a young woman gets on the church radar. Who is she sleeping with? Whose man is she after? What secrets are in her closet? Does her walk align with her talk? Men do not face the same type of scrutiny. If so, the gender distribution of ministerial roles would not be so skewed in their favor. Male ministers are afforded the liberty to be far more scandalous.

Misogyny is very prevalent in the Black church and has become an accepted norm. A close friend at Duke was pursuing marriage counseling from a very prominent Black religious scholar on the faulty at the university while I attended. She unnervingly recounted to me how he propositioned her and used lewd language during their individual sessions. I could not believe it. My shock was not because he had a reputation as such a paragon of virtue. Rather, it was because he was old, fat, and decrepit while she was a vibrant twentysomething. What would he have done with it if she broke him off a piece? At the same time, I had no reason to doubt her. We learned later that he had a pattern of such behavior.

Since accepting my call to ministry, I have become a frequent target of predatory men as an unattached single woman. Most of them were married and looking for someone who also had to be discreet with their affairs. It was no aberration to have my face licked, neck kissed, butt grabbed, breasts mashed, or a groin thrust against me during so-called church hugs. These acts took place at locations far and wide. They are not particular to a culture or sect. It is hard to avoid them without making a scene. My mother raised me never to make a scene in public. I think I need to start making scenes.

Harassment occurs overtly as well. Rev. used to speak to me inappropriately while appearing to the casual onlooker to be within the bounds of propriety. On the last occasion, I was sitting on the other side of his executive-sized desk immediately after service. He was surrounded by shelves filled with books he had never read. The stated purpose was a progress report over Christmas break during my second year of seminary. I recounted the classes I completed that semester and the respective grades earned with my ankles crossed and hands clasped in my lap.

Rev. swirled toward me in his high-back leather chair, leaned in and said, "You think you can escape me all the way down there in Atlanta? I was there recently and started to look you up while out painting town red with my sons in ministry."

"Where did you dine? Or did you take in a show or go shopping?" I asked.

"We went to strip clubs" he winked and replied with his raspy voice. "You'd be surprised at what some women will do for a few bills."

A middle-aged female member of the ministerial staff covered her mouth snickering at his remarks as she passed his open office door to retrieve her purse from the attached conference room. Rev. leaned back and smiled like The Grinch as he took pleasure in my discomfort. At that point, it became clear this man could in no way lead me spiritually. I grabbed my belongings and left abruptly without saying a word. That was the last time I interacted with him.

German chancellor Otto von Bismarck is attributed with saying "There are two things you don't want to see being made—sausage and legislation." I hereby submit a third: preachers. Being corrupt to the core, it was important for old player preachers like Rev. to groom aspiring young ministers to be as much of a spawn of Satan as they are. That way, the others cannot call them out on their actions.

Some seasoned ministers make it their business to ensure the end product is not too clean. First, they line up all the sexual favors a new candidate can stand. They have men's fellowship at strip clubs. Alcohol and drug abuse are no strangers within these circles. The best advice for separating people from their money, running women, controlling minds, or whatever the individual's chosen vice is proffered freely. Once they indoctrinate their subjects into the game, the ministers cannot be held accountable by them. You see, there is no honor among thieves. Female ministers become prey, especially to disqualify them as competition. An irony of all ironies is that keeping their noses clean becomes a liability for ministers because their peers have nothing to hold over their heads.

Friends and I used to jokingly refer to the predominantly Black Interdenominational Theological Center across town in Atlanta as "pimp finishing school." Some of the male graduates left just as jacklegged as they arrived. They invested more in mastering the game than earning their Master of Divinity by not seizing the opportunities available to be equipped fully for professional ministry. It was no coincidence that the time I was preparing for ministry also coincided with a significant number of drug dealers leaving the trade for a legal hustle in the pulpit.

Carter G. Woodson wrote so presciently in 1933:

> Because the Negro church is such a free field and it is controlled largely by the Negroes themselves, it seems that practically all the incompetents and undesirables who have been barred from other walks of life by race prejudice and economic difficulties have rushed into the ministry for the exploitation of the people. Honest ministers who are trying to do their duty, then, find their task made difficult by these men who stoop to practically everything conceivable. Almost anybody of the lowest type may get into the Negro ministry.[20]

As much as my classmates walked in the light by day, many crept by the dark of night as much as those in secular academic programs. True to Rev.'s warnings, rumors started flying that I was a lesbian because my rakish male classmates could not score with me. My lesbian classmates came after me subsequently with even less success. Many of the twentysomething crowd had not yet mastered their domain sexually and were still sowing their wild oats. Quite a few of the more mature students were divorcees testing the waters again. There were also married ones stepping out on spouses they left back home. Do not get me started on the experimental homosexuals or those sleeping with their married pastors. The campus apartments allotted for seminarians were always abuzz with gossip. What made it all so scandalous was that most were projecting an image different from their reality. Fortunately, I lived off campus and did not hang out over there.

It was common in the South for men to approach religious women claiming God told them said woman was their wife. Social pressure to be married is pretty intense in that region. It is even more so if either party is in ministry. Some women were gullible enough to take the bait—even if the man had a wife already. Others simply obeyed their thirst. If God had not likewise inspired me, then the conversation was moot. More often than not, the pursuer had no matrimonial intentions. It was just another line in their arsenal to disarm women. I have not heard such lame rap since returning home. Our players have so much more to work with.

The summer of my return home was transformational. I moved back to DC in May 2000 with a diploma that I picked up from the registrar's office after skipping commencement exercises, but no ordination papers. My friends had married, advanced in their careers, and purchased homes. I was 31, unemployed, and sleeping in my childhood bedroom. A series of temp jobs held me down until I was able to find a position in management consulting. Nobody was as hard on me as I was on myself.

I also had not had sex in five years. Every nerve in my body was on end. St. Augustine prayed "O Lord make me chaste, but not yet." I had not added that latter caveat to my petition and thought I was good to go. Celibacy was easy to endure in Atlanta, but I did not stand much of a chance in DC. Black women walking around Atlanta might as well be invisible as far as brothers are concerned. Brothers at home relate better to women. Compliments flowed freely, without being intrusive, as I simply walked down the street or rode the subway. A homeless man once asked me to marry him after I gave him his weekly alms when I worked downtown. I stopped in my tracks and wondered what he would look like cleaned up. He replied, "don't look back or you might get hooked." I had a good laugh, but he eventually disappeared from that corner for good.

The pursuit of ministry was now over and the pendulum was about to swing in a different direction. The summer of 2000 was for me like the liberating season of Rumspringa for Amish teenagers. All the freedom in the world was at hand with the option never to return to the constraints that bound me. I left DC three years prior abstaining from cussing, drinking, and sex. The first two returned to me naturally in Atlanta as outlets for stress. It was time to test the waters with the third.

No longer was I trying to be ostensibly pious or particularly useful. Neither did I approach God with the formality of structured prayers, but rather conversed with my Lord candidly. R&B singer Kina released her debut album that summer including songs capturing my angst. I played it to death as an escape valve for the anger I had been repressing. Reading Washington Post columnist Jill Nelson's womanist manifesto, *Straight, No Chaser: How I Became a Grown-Up Black Woman*, also provided some context for my experience. And I got back in the gym to lose the twenty-five pounds I gained while no one else saw me naked.

It was time to be a singular individual in the world living in God's presence. I did not even feel like the same person anymore. Part of my personality eroded under the stress of my ecclesiastical striving. That sense was lost on me as I dissociated from my reality while living in a strange city for three years and immersing myself in my studies. Returning home brought that stark realization to light. Little did I know, my experience induced a paralytic angst that rendered me unproductive in every aspect of life. Reconciling the always winning woman with the defeated preacher seemed impossible.

Sexual repression was making me neither a better Christian nor a more functional person. (The church would actually be a better place if more people simply got laid). Circulating socially became a struggle. Not only was I approaching the age when women are said to be both at their sexual peak and statistically unlikely to marry, the 500-pound gorilla on my back was raging. Every step I took felt like I was going to spontaneously combust. I dared not advertise that fact lest every player in my orbit would seek to seize it as a trophy. It did not take long before I fell. Not being touched by a man for so long had become disorienting for someone who was used to having her needs met. Since doing everything by the letter did not net me much gain, I threw caution to the wind. My experience with the church made me think my life before was not so bad.

One day toward the end of summer, I stopped past a friend's house after work. He had been trying to get with me for well over a decade with no success. As soon as he began flirting and touching me, my clothes fell off. I had no resistance because I had been out of the game for so long. The sex was wild, hot, and downright animalistic. We hooked up a few more times until I gained a sense of normalcy. He had no idea why he hit the jackpot all of a sudden and I never told him. At least I did not fall into some random hands.

The problem with the church and sexuality is the organization tries to institutionalize one of the most basic of human functions. According to their doctrine, people are not at liberty to be sexually active without the church's sanction. Nowhere in the Bible is sex outside of marriage forbidden categorically. I first asked in Sunday School as a teenager and almost caused my teacher to swallow her tongue. She kept saying "the Bible says…" I asked, "Where?" She began to provide commentary, but could not find a passage that made her point in a straightforward manner. Fornication has been interpreted as such. However, the word has evolved from its meaning at the time of the recording of Scripture. Fornication has been construed in modernity as synonymous with pre-marital sex. The meaning of adultery has also been stretched in an attempt to confine sex to marriage. Scripture unpacks the meaning of adultery in several places, but never goes that far.

Leviticus 18 describes an exhaustive list of prohibitions against particular forms of sexual activity. They range from close and distant family members to barnyard animals. If God wanted to say "do not have sex outside of marriage," it would have been right there. People were getting it on in the Bible within and outside of marital bounds without rebuke. Solomon had 300 concubines. The Lord chastised him only for the ones of foreign origin who turned him to other gods.

As with the Ten Commandments, the Lord forbids extramarital sex in the Sex Codes. Adultery, which is cut and dry, does not receive nearly as much attention within the church as is necessary. Many of the same preachers talking with certainty about gray areas turn a blind eye to the prevalence of married Christians—many of them ministers—stepping out on their covenanted unions. That is not to mention the biblical restrictions on remarriage after divorce. Yet, the loins of single people are governed closely. None of this is to endorse wanton promiscuity. Responsible sexuality requires ethics, but the church does not like to engage in nuanced conversations. "Just do what I say and not what I do" is what they tacitly order.

Billy Graham had a rule that he would not allow himself to be alone with a woman who was not his wife under any circumstances for fear of temptation or accusation. He had been known to even avoid entering an elevator containing only an individual of the fairer sex. Such seems shrewd on the surface, but is hard in practice as women now make up over half of seminary graduates and the majority of church members.

On some occasions, excessive prudishness is a form of over compensation for known philanderers. Their insecure wives are also amusing thinking every woman is on the prowl for their husbands. The reality is he is reaching for women who are often beyond his grasp. Do not give him too much credit. Your husband cannot pull the women you fear. I also find it amazing how men to whom I have never expressed any attraction suddenly need to erect new boundaries when they finally get a woman. Been knowing them for decades and suddenly they think my character has mutated or they have magically become irresistible. Please!

Satirical magazine, *The Onion*, took it to the extreme. "

> Expressing concerns about the propriety of being left alone with a syrup container of the opposite sex, Vice President Mike Pence reportedly asked his waiter Thursday to remove Mrs. Butterworth from the table until his wife arrived to join him at a local diner. He decided even having Mrs. Butterworth within arm's reach could lead him to have impure thoughts.[21]

Why men claiming to be empowered by the Spirit of Christ cannot interact equitably with women like Jesus did is beyond me. Jesus often left his dimwitted disciples wondering why he was speaking with women without male company. Jesus simply went about his ministry with honor and never stopped to explain. Be like Jesus.

The most effective way not to be accused of sexual harassment is to maintain a sense of propriety in the open, as well as behind closed doors, and to cultivate it among one's peers. A male acquaintance who attended a historically Black Samuel DeWitt Proctor School of Theology at Virginia Union University in Richmond, Virginia recounted a pastoral care professor telling him a woman who approaches a male minister always has ulterior motives. I expressed shock that such a sexist sentiment was being propagated in a formal setting. But it did explain how some men have come to develop such a sense of sexual entitlement.

That same acquaintance happened to be the only preacher I have ever dated. My post-seminary funk was still in full effect, so I was in a bad place. He was somebody I would not have given the time of day previously as he was a grifter is search of a woman to elevate him. We first met when I was an undergrad and in the throes of my days as a party girl. When we reconnected the year following my return from Atlanta, he claimed to need assistance with his studies as he was starting his ministerial journey. Being idle with a very expensive theology degree, I was happy to oblige. Well, one thing led to another and we were together almost daily for six months.

Turns out this psycho not only had a girlfriend who was a professor several states away in Michigan, but asked her to marry him while we were dating. It blew my mind that he had the time for another because he smothered me. I could not get in the house from work good before he was at my door. He also called me fifty-thousand times a day "checking in." It was revealed later that I unknowingly drove him to the airport when he went away to his engagement party. He expressed disappointment at the time because I dropped him off curbside rather than accompanying him into the terminal. One Sunday after church, he informed me over brunch that he was getting married as if sharing the most mundane news. The shock was so disorienting that I could not even navigate my way home from the restaurant where we dined frequently.

My brother took his little sister getting played very personally. He schooled me on all matters concerning the game of romance before I began dating. Although we spoke regularly and commuted together daily, I never mentioned my misgivings about my suitor until after his disclosure. It was not as if I had not noticed the red flags; it was more so that I felt powerless to avoid them. When I ended things, he said wistfully "my getting married has nothing to do with us." I looked at him puzzled and verbally undressed him. He added with tears in his eyes, "I can't believe you're breaking up with me just because I'm getting married." Dude had no intention on being faithful. Then he stole my well-marked study Bible as a parting gesture.

We worshipped together on several occasions at the historic Shiloh Baptist Church in DC where he was a lifelong member. It counted the likes of Civil Rights icon Dorothy Height, political scientist Ron Walters, and many other luminaries as members. His pastor refused to speak to me or shake my extended hand after service. The Dean of his seminary treated me with the same dismissiveness when we went to hear him preach at Rankin Chapel. Rather than outing their charge's philandering, they behaved as if I were the dishonest cheater. On the flip side, his mother was very nice to me the times we visited her home, although she never mentioned the existence of another love interest. Women in my family do not enable such trifling behavior.

In the game of the Black church, the man can do no wrong. With the community of educated Blacks having only one degree of separation, his fiancé and I had mutual acquaintances. She found out he was running game on her and married him anyway. As I licked my wounds after learning of his deceit, one of my sisters in ministry scolded me. "You know we are not supposed to date them anyway!" That snapped me back to my senses. It is not that every preacher is rotten, but they exist in an environment that supports their worst inclinations with little to no accountability. Like the survivors of the Holocaust, I said "never again."

In July of 2003, one of my new neighbors passed away. His wife was a longtime member of Allen Chapel. Although I knew them well and we had a strong sense of community, I was torn about attending the funeral. There was no reasonable excuse for missing the services. As a matter of fact, I was raised to attend a funeral unless you have a really good reason not to do so. Nothing says "I love you" like being there for someone during their time of bereavement. My initial plan was simply to pay my respects during the viewing and leave. My stomach tightened and I broke out in a cold sweat as I entered the sanctuary.

Another neighbor spotted me walking down the aisle looking uneasy after greeting the family and beckoned me to sit with our block's delegation. I felt safe. Although the church did not protect me, people in my life organically did. Rev. was waiting for me in the vestibule after the service as I exited the sanctuary. We stood face-to-face staring each other up and down silently like contending prizefighters. The battleground was my soul.

An amazing thing happened one Friday evening in September a couple of years later. That is the time when the Black bourgeoisie from around the world gathers in Washington to blow smoke and put on airs. The formal name is the Congressional Black Caucus Annual Legislative Conference, but it is a straight-up, pretentious, see-and-be-seen bacchanalia. By day, we celebrate the accomplishments of Black members of Congress, state and local officials, advocates, academicians, and business people. It feels good to acknowledge our collective greatness in a world that continually tries to negate it. I can bear witness that not much redemptive happens there after dark, but it is a good time. After a couple of days of attending the perfunctory workshops and networking, the festivities were in full swing.

I was in the lobby of a swanky downtown hotel dressed in sexy finery and waiting for my friends to arrive so we could join the party circuit around town. In the distance, I spotted a group of Rev.'s scandalous sons in ministry gathered in a circle with cocktails in hand. As I approached them to say hello, I noticed an older man breaking away from the crowd. As he made haste, I recognized him as the one and only. I was surprisingly happy to see him and exclaimed "Hey Rev.!" He took no chances on an angry confrontation and got away before I could extend an embrace. Then, I had an epiphany: I was so over what he had done to me.

How I came to forgive him, I do not know. It was not just the alcohol talking either. My heart was unburdened and spirit unfettered. It was seemingly a gift I was able to receive once I stopped trying to correct the past. A door opened that never really was shut.

7

INSTITUTIONAL INVESTMENTS

The finest qualities of our nature, like the bloom on fruits,
can be preserved only by the most delicate handling.

Walt Whitman

The preceding events led me to wonder how evil is so prevalent in a space that is supposed to be holy. Being a management consultant by profession, I think a lot about the church as an institution rather than the symbolic body of Christ. How did we get where we are? What do we truly espouse? What role am I playing in it all?

The early church came to be defined in sociological terms as a cult. Cults have gotten a bad rap due to events that have taken place in some extreme forms. However, the church was indeed a cult during the first few centuries of existence. Its formation revolved around a charismatic leader with fixed boundaries, rigid teaching, and communal living. That fits the modern definition perfectly.

Adherence to Jesus' teachings and a firm belief in his resurrection were the criteria for membership. The social isolation of leaving families of origin and even established societies made membership more cultish. Converts changed their entire identity for another. Jews left—if they had not already been expelled from—the synagogue. Others likewise abandoned their established religions and social circles to wholly adapt to the requirements of this new sect.

The early church was all about social control, as is almost every community of faith. Social control is essential for maintaining boundaries and financing the operation. It was true then and even more so now. Reading much of the New Testament presents an "us versus them" duality. The first-generation church lived under grave threat of persecution and heresy and thus went to great lengths to protect their boundaries.

Some believers like to think they are persecuted for their faith today, but blood is seldom shed in modern American society for the sake of what one believes. Just because you are ostracized does not equate with persecution. Maybe it is because you are unbearable. Consider that. The first converts were slaughtered simply for professing Jesus as Lord. Therefore, they had to take measures to protect one another while still discipling the world. A lot was at stake to maintain the movement and the integrity of its teachings.

Institutions by nature are rigid, controlling, and soulless. They are all about conformity to their norms and preservation of their existence. Some examples are government agencies, universities, corporations, and large charitable organizations. Max Weber held that "bureaucracy, the rational spirit's organizational manifestation, was so efficient and powerful a means of controlling men and women that, once established, the momentum of bureaucratization was irreversible."[22] Hence, so many well-intentioned organizations have drifted away from their original purpose, far beyond the point of no return.

We have a saying in management consulting: Activity does not always equal productivity. In other words, just because an entity is doing something does not mean they are working toward their stated mission or goals. Busy is often the enemy of the good. Just because they are actively engaged does not mean they are doing the right things—even according to their own standards.

Institutions exist to serve a specific purpose and take great measures to maintain their character. People rely on them to deliver what they promise often throughout vast enterprises. Competition demands they do so consistently. Problems arise when the institution's character comes into conflict with its mission. More often than not, preservation of the institution prevails over adhering to mission or core values. It is a wrap once an organization reaches that tipping point, but that does not stop the show from going on. Individuals and organizations of bad character often cloak themselves in good works just as Satan likes to parade as an angel of light.

The first change the early church had to make was to establish itself as distinct from Judaism. Jesus was a Jew as were most of his followers. However, Jesus had followers who were not Jews. The descending of the Holy Spirit at Pentecost unified believers in faith. Not long thereafter, divisions arose between those who were previously Jews and those who were Gentiles. The Apostle Paul addressed the need to reinterpret the law in light of the grace of the gospel in the book of Galatians, but the actual implementation occurred over time and off the record.

During the first few centuries, church membership began after an encounter with the risen Christ, which baptism followed. Either you were in or you were out. There was no room for seekers. Catechism was the context in which teaching took place and thus became the nurturing ground for those exploring the faith. They were more accessible. Only fully-converted believers were supposedly included in worship and leadership. And they were scrutinized. Once accepted, the behavioral norms became well-defined. Living up to those standards was not easy. Those indwelled by the Holy Spirit were validated by their fruit.

There comes a time in every organization's life when change becomes necessary. Institutions resist change by their very nature. A leading reason is the nature of the change. Was it autonomous or involuntary? It is one thing to go through a grueling internal process which usually results in small, incremental changes. It is entirely another to have radical change forced upon the organization by external forces. The latter produces the greatest resistance not because of the change itself, but because the manner in which it is imposed presents a sense of loss of control.

Think about desegregation in America. The federal government could have ordered it sweepingly and quickly. However, the Supreme Court included "with all deliberate speed" in its Brown v. Board of Education decision. That phrase removed the force of law for advancing racial equality with allowances for subjective discretion. That is also not to mention how institutional racism is engrained every facet of American life. Dismantling white supremacy still remains a challenge today because so many have a vested interest in maintaining it.

Sometimes organizations resist recommendations and mandates reflexively to protect the status quo from unnecessary change. That raises the question, however, of who gets to decide whether change is necessary. The church tends to be extremely vested in stagnation for the same reason secular institutions are. However, the body of Christ is called not to be conformed to the patterns of this world. The church is a living organism not a machine. Rigidity impedes the work of the Holy Spirit which represents God as change agent.

The task of management consultants is to advise leaders on standardizing processes around an organization's stated mission and aligning resources in the most efficient manner. We sometimes forget the church is a business. As such, it has operations to oversee and bills to pay. Therefore, it must produce a consistent product. Standardization is essential when selling a physical product; it can be an impediment when overemphasized or misapplied in the invisible realm.

Institutions stifle creativity and can become mental prisons. Even when they are supposedly undergoing transformation, institutions retain consultants to preserve the status quo through change management. The Holy Spirit who is supposed to be the guiding force of the church cannot be controlled like the elements of an industrial enterprise. Change comes eventually with or without the church's consent. Resistance takes the form of internal politics, social control, and downright disobedience. Allowing rank and file members to see the bowels that restrict its movements is bad for business. Once exposed, the organization is more prone to plug its butt than take an enema.

The institutional church's consistent emphasis on the temporal at the expense of the invisible has been an obstacle for centuries. See how easy it was to effect change at Pentecost. Unless we start prioritizing the dynamic nature of the Holy Spirit, the church will remain vested in the status quo. The more the church obsesses with fundraising, doctrine, and good form, the less it will be relevant to the people who need it most. So what if an idea is not pragmatic. God is always doing new things that appear absurd to the flesh. Evil lurks so freely in Christendom because we often deny the power within us individually and collectively. Releasing the restraints is not as hard as it seems because we cannot package wind anyway.

The typical pastor has not a clue about the disposition of the souls of their congregants, but they can attest to church attendance, lifestyle, and financial contributions. If preaching the deceased into heaven were their responsibility, most folks would be in trouble. Rare is the eulogy where the preacher can honestly testify to the quality of the spiritual life of the deceased and bless the memory of it. Usually, it's more like a generic Mad Libs template with "insert name here" printed under blank lines at defined intervals. In the same manner, denominational leaders assess congregations on their membership rolls, finances, and activities. These are not God's performance metrics.

Thinking about how much I had poured into the church financially and otherwise caused me much consternation. Those investments were not returning much to me tangibly or intangibly. As much as we were at odds, my membership was valued more as a number on the respective rolls, in addition to the monetary and in-kind contributions, than anything I brought spiritually. Hence, I left and did not miss anything during my absences. My warm body and checkbook are welcome back, but not the invisible substance that is most vital to the body.

One day in Bible study, the discussion got stuck on multiple understandings of a particular passage in the gospel of John. A closer reading did not reveal much in the various versions of the Bible we were using. I promised to go home and translate it from the original Greek text and return with an acceptable range of interpretations. This was not terribly hard because Johannine writings tend to be the simplest linguistically. The greatest difficulty would have resulted from the fact that over a decade had passed since I last used those skills. Surprisingly, it came back to me with ease.

The teacher clasped her hands in front of her chest and marveled with a smile. "It's so nice to have such a resource available to us for free."

"This knowledge did not come for free; I paid a lot for it." I quipped. The class nodded knowingly as they were aware of my credentials. Then I appropriated a familiar hymn tongue-in-cheek singing, "Must Dionne bear the cost alone and all the church go free?" They stared blankly.

Then I got to thinking about how Jesus' teachings were the furthest thing from the authoritarian institution we know today. First, his mission to his followers was simple. Love. Teach. Obey. He fulfilled the law, introduced no hierarchy, asked no one for money, and built not one single edifice. Contrast that with how the church has invested its time and resources throughout the centuries since his death and resurrection. The institution has convinced us we need it for more than we do simply to maintain the heft of its overhead. Ministers induce demand for their services in the same manner car salespersons push paint protectant. The consumer does not need it as much as the seller's bottom line does. Imagine how the integrity of preaching and ministry would improve if those doing so were financially independent from their consumers.

Think of churches like hospitals. In this era of health reform, heavy emphasis is being placed on ensuring patients are treated in the most cost-effective setting. Inpatient acute care is the most resource-intensive and hence the most expensive setting. My hometown and most of America have a decades-long crisis of people going to the emergency department for minor conditions. A large portion are uninsured or covered publicly by Medicaid or Medicare. That means their medical expenses typically get passed on to others. We have to find ways to change their consumption patterns to optimize resource allocation and utilization within the overall delivery system.

Most believers and seekers do not require inpatient, acute spiritual care. Over-consumption of religion—whether voluntarily or involuntarily—is akin to locking a person in an asylum. In our society, people are institutionalized involuntarily when they are a threat to themselves, a threat to others, or unable to care for themselves. Individuals can also commit themselves voluntarily when they feel unsafe, are a threat to someone or society, or are a danger to themselves. Are these the conditions under which discipleship should be administered? Imagine how many more works of love could be performed without so much bureaucracy and overhead.

This begs the question of what the fear is of having believers out freely bearing witness to the world. Once they are duly equipped, why is there a perceived need to keep them all bound? Jesus consistently sent his followers forward. His final words before his ascension solidified that charge. *Go therefore and [teach] all of the nations, baptizing them in the name of the Father and of the Son and of the Holy Spirit.* Missionary work—both local and foreign—is an isolated and episodic affair in most of the church. Rather, the bulk of what passes for discipleship is self-perpetuating to keep members contained and controlled. We cannot put another in a cell without imprisoning ourselves.

A seminary professor and I had a conversation about my struggle during one of my return visits a few years after graduation. He was orphaned at a young age and joined a Catholic monastic order after he aged out of the children's home. People tend to idealize his history as a monk, but he described that time in his life as very oppressive. He told me, "you do not have to professionalize your faith" and described how he savors his freedom. Those words were as liberating as confounding. I asked him, "Why did you not tell me sooner?"

Never during the two semesters I studied New Testament with him or our many personal conversations did he mention this gnostic secret. Do not get me wrong. I received stellar theological training and have not a single regret about pursuing it. The problem is it was all from the perspective of being of service to the institution. Then I asked God, "What am I supposed to do with this expensive degree?"

I read years later that:

> Seminary training isn't supposed to be about preparation for a nice, cushy desk job. Neither is it supposed to be about preparation for decades of chaplaincy to congregations that want to be tended and serviced, not served and led. What if, for the next couple decades anyway, seminaries became more like entrepreneurial boot camps than shop management schools?[23]

I have come to realize that reinforcing my faith through education equipped me for a higher level of being in the world and not simply the career change I expected. One cannot put a price on that experience, but we will have to if anyone wants to employ it.

Another professor and I were chatting in his office as I was preparing to graduate from seminary. He happened to be the director of the Black

Church Studies program, but we had limited contact. I explained to him that having grown up in an almost exclusively Black community, steeped in African Methodism, and studying Afro-American Studies as an undergrad, I did not feel the need to focus on Black religion in seminary. This sealed for me how my faith transcended my cultural identity, although the latter remains the context in which I exercise the former.

We then got to talking about my experience with sexual harassment in the AME church. He looked at me askance and said, "Is that why I have never seen you smile?" His response astounded me as I had no idea how I had been facing the world. Many of my classmates and I reconnected on social media a decade after graduation. They too have remarked at what a different person I am now. Hearing these observations forced me to perform some self-examination. I allowed my circumstances to deprive me of the pleasure of relating more meaningfully to my classmates. The strangest irony is that I still had joy. My relationship with God remained uninterrupted as I wrestled with the institution claiming to embody the divine's presence in the world.

Fortunately, this conversation occurred during my last semester at Emory and I would be returning home in a few weeks. In a sense I had been walking around like a battered wife. Abusers control the minds of their victims by directing them:

> Don't talk.
> Don't trust.
> Don't feel.
> Pretend like nothing is happening.

That is exactly how I navigated the world as Rev. and I engaged in interpersonal and spiritual warfare. We would exchange fiery words in his office, but act like everything was copacetic the moment we walked into public space. He assured me he was working on a special way for me to bypass the ordination process. No other candidates from our congregation or the Washington Annual Conference received similar treatment. Why was I so different? I hedged my bets initially just in case there was a grain of truth to what he was telling me. Rev. would get my hopes up with false updates on my progress only to let me down each time I was not complicit with one of his demands. Now, I had crapped out.

My final semester ended and I was homeward bound. My best friend from seminary called me after exams.

"So, what are you up to these days?" she inquired.

"Packing."

"You really are serious about putting this experience behind you?"

"Absolutely," I replied as I wrapped dishes in newspaper and stacked them neatly in boxes.

It was time to get a dose of some old-time religion.

The early church was an intimate affair. Worship was typically held in homes around the dinner table. The primary reason was because it was an underground movement existing as a threat to the prevailing political power. Once Constantine made Christianity the official religion of the Roman Empire in the Fourth Century, the nature of the church changed dramatically. Most significantly, persecution stopped. What was previously a scandalous choice became the option of the most respectable. If I start a church, we will be returning to our scandalous roots.

The church within the Empire took on the pomp and pageantry of the state, not to mention the bureaucracy. Ministry became a job akin to civil service rather than a sacrificial way of life shared by all believers. Some church leaders were offered actual government positions of religious import. Such sinecures were offered as a form of political patronage with little to no redeeming value. A person cannot disrupt the world order if they are preoccupied with mindless work.

Constantine built churches with the character of Roman temples, but also remained well-acquainted with paganism. Church leaders tacitly accepted his compromised support, although Constantine did not technically become a Christian until he was baptized on his deathbed.[24] Who, dare I ask, performed said baptism? Constantine was declared a pagan god after his death.

Christendom today resembles a cross between Neo-Judaism and the Roman Empire more than it does the early church. It is very non-reflective and self-satisfied as was the church at Laodicea in the book of Revelation. Any discontent with the church's bureaucracy or its relationships with the established world order is squashed immediately. Religious leaders covet and take delight in getting invited to princely palaces to rub elbows with government leaders, as well as in their knowledge of polity. Those relationships are maintained to keep prophecy in check.

The first movement within the church in response to Roman infiltration was to pursue life away from organized religion. My first semester church history class opened with an overview of the first Christian monastics. I had heard of monasticism as an individual endeavor, but this was my first introduction to its origins as a movement. Extracting myself from the excrement in which I had become mired required a deliberate reshaping of my practice of faith.

As my final semester drew to a close, I began to reflect on the value of my education overall in light of my estranged relationship with the church. Without pursuing theological training apart from the church, I would have crumbled under the weight of our separation. My studies helped me to deconstruct the historic, sociological, psychological, and theological underpinnings of my experience. However, my studies did not resolve the existential pain.

Although I visited the predominantly-white Oak Grove United Methodist Church near my apartment frequently after I left the AME Church, I did not establish much of a connection. The pastor was the protégé of famed preacher Fred Craddock and bore the distinction well. The messages seemed tailored to getting me through the fallout, although he knew nothing about my predicament. The warm fellowship kept me from getting too jaded. I stood out as one of only a handful of Black attendees so people were extra nice to me. Their demographics were quite remarkable as this was a large congregation by any measure. Remaining almost all white takes a lot of work for a church in Atlanta in this day and age. Atlanta is America's Black mecca and the neighborhood was racially and culturally diverse. Nevertheless, my days in the city were numbered so I needed to plan my next move.

Graduation was bittersweet and not an occasion to which I was looking forward. The fact that I would no longer be in a religious environment most of my waking hours was appealing. The fact that I had to find a way to repay all the debt I incurred pursuing theological training was daunting. My parents paid for my undergraduate education and I worked part-time to cover my living expenses. I received a scholarship paired with an assistantship for my first master's degree, borrowing only a small amount for living expenses.

My approach to this program was different. Although the school awarded me a partial scholarship, I incurred student loans to cover the remainder of my tuition and expenses. My debt load was three times the level of my previous master's degree. I wanted to focus intensely on my studies as my goal at the time was to proceed directly into a PhD program in systematic theology. My grades were better than either my undergraduate or previous graduate program because of my drive, discipline, and sense of purpose. Had I known how the church would turn on me, I certainly would not have taken such a huge risk.

By providence or coincidence, I received a mailing for a retreat sponsored by the Friends of St. Benedict. More than likely, my name was added to their mailing list from being a supporter of the Washington National Cathedral where they are based. Reading the brochure was compelling despite the closest one geographically coinciding with commencement. I was near the end of my funds for the semester, but wanted to take the leap. My mother and I discussed it during our weekly phone conversations and my parents agreed to pay for it.

While my classmates were preparing to celebrate, I was trying to make sense of my last three years. I thought I came to seminary for a career change, but a job in the church was the last thing I desired at that point. What to do following my studies never crossed my mind because I assumed an additional degree would follow. My psyche was too scarred to consider undertaking another academic load. The application packages for doctoral programs remained stacked on my desk without so much as my name entered on the forms. A season of quiet contemplation apart from my striving seemed in order.

The drive from Atlanta to a small town outside Asheville, North Carolina was scenic and soothing. My CD changer played a series of gospel albums as my mind cleared to make room for a new vision from God. It never dawned on me how out of my natural habitat I would be. The conference center was on 1,400 acres in the Blue Ridge Mountains with winding hiking paths leading to a large lake at its center. As a city slicker who refused even to attend summer camp, living remotely with no radio, television, phone, or computers was foreign. All of the other participants were white, affluent, Episcopalian, and old enough to be my parent if not grandparent. However, I have seldom felt such a deep communion. Only a few were clergy, but they did not differentiate themselves from the rest of us.

A Benedictine Experience is a type of retreat during which participants live like its namesake monks for a week. The guiding principle is to abide by the balance of prayer, work, study, and rest in community. We awakened and ate breakfast in silence, only conversing after the first of seven worship events during the day. Being able to keep my mouth shut was the greatest perceived challenge on the front-end. It came easier than I thought and bred an enduring appreciation for silent contemplation.

The order of each day was very structured. We were silent most of the time. Otherwise, we were engaged in seven periods of devotion, between which fell some form of manual labor, reading or lecture, and leisure. Each activity was punctuated by a period of silence or meditation. *The Rule of St. Benedict* directs one to end an action before starting another. Activities must not adjoin one another to ensure mindfulness in the moment. A period of rest is required between them to release oneself. That applies not only to discrete daily tasks, but also larger endeavors of life.

I had an even higher experience with the Lord's Supper during the Benedictine Experience as we celebrated the Eucharist daily. The difference was we actually drank from a common cup like Jesus and his disciples, which my mother sealed in my mind at an early age never to do with anyone. Although everyone else seemed accustomed to this practice, I found myself thinking of creative ways to avoid partaking in this part of the rite. The first time the chalice was passed to me, a calm came over my spirit. I closed my eyes, threw my head back and took a deep breath. With my lips barely touching the rim, I sipped. It only took a moment, but felt like an eternity. Immediately, I felt closer to my brothers and sisters sharing the experience. The rest of the week was nothing short of transformative and nobody caught typhoid fever.

We all shared a good laugh at my utter shock at the fact we consumed alcoholic beverages during our recreational activities at the end of the day. Episcopalians are one of the few denominations to imbibe openly while gathered. I joked that they were only doing visibly what some other sects run to the trunk of their cars to do. That certainly took the edge off and put me at ease with a group with whom I would have never interacted organically on such an intimate level. This opened us up to real talk about our respective journeys and current situations from which we each sought respite.

The Benedictine Experience certainly attained its goal of cultivating a sense of mindfulness and deepening my practice of faith. The key distinction is that it is temporary in nature just like all mountaintop experiences. Participants returned to their respective homes and congregations never to convene again as a group. As we were checking out, one of the participants shared how inspired she was by my fortitude.

"I am excited about what God is going to do through you. What are your plans?" she asked.

"I have no plans."

She uttered, "You are going to start a church."

"No, I'm not!" I rebutted.

I left that thought right there in Asheville, or so I thought. One of my college friends asked me when I was going to start a church every time he saw me for many years to come, without any knowledge of the above exchange. It was eerie, to say the least.

The ride home was different from the journey there. My normal instinct is to crank up the stereo soon after I start the ignition. This time, I slid into the driver's seat and glided all the way from Western North Carolina to Atlanta, Georgia in silent bliss. God felt present with me in a different way as I had learned to listen from deep within without regard to environment or circumstances. It was as if I had been through spiritual detox.

Therefore, the end of my theological studies brought me full-circle to my introduction to the singularity of faith at the beginning of my first semester. Seminary was a purifying experience that strengthened my footing during an intense spiritual conflict. I did not appreciate it for such at the time, but have come to cherish the education my grandfather always encouraged me to pursue because nobody could ever take it away. I continued to study with the Friends of St. Benedict for a couple of years after I returned to DC until I found fellowship with a congregation I could call home.

The Benedictine Experience was foundational for personalizing my faith and eventually becoming a fully deinstitutionalized believer. It allowed me the breathing room to detach from my past experience with the church and to stop trying to control my future. Looking for God's presence in every moment, every praise, every interaction, and even in nature helped me to become mindful of how the institutional church did not have a hold on the divine.

Institutions have value. Dorothy Height had a saying she used frequently. "If I take a finger and touch you, you won't even know you've been tapped. If I take two fingers, you will know that something touched you. But if I bring all of those fingers together in a fist, I can give you a terrible blow!" We can accomplish far more collectively than we can alone.

There is strength in numbers. However, we are not to confine our living or our practice of faith to institutions. My studies revealed significant problems with abuse within all types of faith communities throughout history that manifest whenever people organize. That has nothing to do with God. It has everything to do with human nature.

Humanity puts the insanity in Christianity. The church was crazy from the beginning and always will be. Members of the church at Corinth were rich in gifts, but getting drunk at the communion table. Ecumenical Councils where early church leaders gathered to discuss regulations and theology were contentious to say the least. Hazing even occurred in monasteries. That is not to mention centuries of crusades, inquisitions, witch hunts, colonization, enslavement, genocide, and oppression undertaken supposedly for the cause of Christ.

Despite these things—or even because of them—clear-thinking and regenerated souls must stop the patients from running the asylum. We do not have to play by the rules that led to the current state of affairs. This is not to say we abandon communities of faith. However, we do not have to be hobbled by them either. Breaking away, even for just a season, is not a total repudiation of organized religion. Rather, it represents freeing oneself to focus on more of God than an institution can hold.

8

THE MAD DASH

*Our faith and our friendships are not shattered by one big act,
but by many small neglects.*

J. Gustav White

It is a fact of life that all relationships end—either by evolution, distance, betrayal, or death. Childhood friends, high school sweethearts, college roommates, sorority sisters and fraternity brothers, spouses, and others we expect to be with us until the end come and go. If we knew then what we know now, what sacrifices we would not have made? What confidences we would not have shared? What commitments we would not have engaged? When all those investments—emotional and otherwise—come up against the inevitable demise, it begs the question: When do you know it is time for the grand finale?

Terminating church membership is very complicated. More than likely, family and social ties led us to overstay the fruitfulness of the relationship. Membership there might have been productive at another point in time, but the marginal spiritual benefit tends to trend downward after a while. A slow spiritual decline seems preferable to searching for a new congregation after the point of recognizing the current one is no longer working.

I can recall being stuck at more than one congregation. Attendance became not just routine, but perfunctory. I would dread the entire affair, but felt obligated on some level. When my view of the church and experience with God evolved, it was time for a change.

I actually enjoyed being a member of Allen Chapel, the church I was attending when I discerned my call to ministry. The worship style was more Charismatic than my childhood congregation and Bible studies were engaging and plentiful. I grew a lot in the few years I was there. It was during this time that I took the initiative to read Scripture in its entirety. Ironically, most Christians invest a lot of time in the machine, but never take the time to read the manual.

My friends and classmates back in Atlanta wondered why I did not just leave the denomination and shop for another church while completing my theological studies. That made sense on the surface because I could have been ordained by graduation. However, I identified as much with the social and political roots of the AME Church as I did with its theology. I also had never been a quitter and was not going to let Rev. win. Besides, the same God who had been leading me thus far would have to direct me to leave. I had a mind to see how the drama would play out and turn into a testimony.

God loves drama. There certainly is no mistaking that the book we hold sacred is known appropriately as the greatest story ever told. Look at what God permitted in human history to allow God's plan for redemption to unfold. As a matter of fact, I had no more need for soap operas after I became serious about studying the Scriptures.

God and I had drama. No fewer than a hundred times did people tell me at different points in my life that I should be preaching. Ministry did not suit my self-image so I ignored them unswervingly. Then God awakened me from the dark of night with an experience too cataclysmic for words. It shook me to my core. I responded in faith by accepting the call, quitting my job, and moving away to attend seminary.

United Methodist preacher Dean Snyder said in a sermon that:

> God only uses a sledgehammer when our defenses are really, really thick. God doesn't use a sledgehammer to crack open a walnut. If you've experienced a weird, supernatural, obviously miraculous prophecy in your life, it is not a compliment. It is not because you have a special gift. It is because you have a special denseness.

It would make for good narrative if I could say every day afterward became easy as Sunday morning. God and I went from sublime intimacy and speaking constantly to cold distance and prolonged periods of silence. Having the gifts of discernment and prophecy, it was not unusual for God to drop a word in my spirit. I had answers to questions I dared not even ask. That was quite a privilege.

Here I was thinking I was special for so many years because God revealed Godself to me in such a powerful way to reorder my world. The experience turned me into a spiritual drama queen. There have been other times since then when I heard what I wanted to hear in matters big and small. I needed an ecstatic, overwhelming experience to compel me to take leaps of faith from that point forward. Snyder said further:

> Many of us try to protect ourselves from hearing a word
> from God. For many of us life is demanding enough,
> uncontrollable enough, without God speaking a word of
> new possibility to us.

I have taken enough lumps to force me to tune my spiritual receptors to determine when God is speaking. Just as in earthly relationships, the need for drama is not healthy. Recall the story of Elijah in 1 Kings 19:11-14. God ordered Elijah to wait on a personal encounter with the divine on the mountain. First came a mighty wind that split the mountain, then an earthquake, then a fire. God was not in either. Then came a still small voice that revealed the message from the Lord.

On the upside, history shows a strong correlation between a dramatic call experience and the object's impact on history. The Apostle Paul, Joan of Arc, and Harriet Tubman are good examples. A little drama can light a fire, keep things interesting, and compel one to do things that do not come naturally. Addiction to drama is counterproductive and creates an environment ripe for dysfunction and abuse in both the spiritual and temporal realms.

So, there I stood waiting not on a violent wind or the earthquake or fire as the only means for hearing from on high. They can be God's means for breaking you down before building you up. The still small voice held the answer. Besides, I want to be found on the right side of the one who said *If you love Me, you will keep My commandments.* He deserves no less.

The end of my second year was when the church would have ordained me had my candidacy not been derailed. I held out for hope even until the week of Annual Conference. Then, I became physically ill of biblical proportions. My face erupted with bumps and boils, my hair began to fall out, my weight increased without explanation, and I hemorrhaged for twelve weeks.

I suffered in silence until one day the pain got so bad, I was doubled-over and could barely walk. This required long-overdue medical attention. My summer job at a software company did not provide leave, but making it through another day like this was not an option. I sent my supervisor an email and walked erect long enough to make it to my car without bringing attention to my discomfort. This was pain like I had never felt before.

The attending physician was dumbfounded during my examination. She felt my uterus contracting repeatedly without any contents to expel. Neither she nor anyone else on duty had ever seen anything like it. They went through a checklist of potential causes, performing both a pregnancy test and endometrial biopsy to screen for uterine cancer. Nothing I said could convince them I had been celibate for years so they insisted on the former. Too many other patients had come through previously claiming to be abstinent, but were totally knocked up. There is something bone-chilling about being told you might have cancer, especially when you are thirty, a picture of health, lost a peer to the disease a year ago almost to the date, and are on edge already. After all I had been through over the previous three years, I cried out to God like the Moses. *So if You are going to deal with me this way, please kill me now.* I always thought I would die young anyway. Not knowing how I would meet my earthly end was anxiety-inducing.

Fortunately, all results were negative. My medical team said they ruled out all potential causes and there was nothing else they could do. A female nurse held my hand, looked me in the eye, and asked plaintively whether I was under any stress. I returned her gaze with a straight face and said "no" with all sincerity so as not to mar the image of the church. Why I felt the need to protect an institution that could not care less about me made no sense. Doing so locked me firmly into the process of somatization in which psychological distress is unconsciously expressed physically. The symptoms represented my physiological response to the stress as I pretended to be unaffected by my invisible injuries at the hands of the church.

When I returned to my apartment, I knew what I had to do. The stress had become toxic and was literally killing me. My body was consuming itself, hence the manifestation of the psychosomatic effects. I wrote The Right Reverend a fiery letter. I had to hit him with his own shtick to expose the church's hypocrisy. The closing said "In the spirit of Richard Allen and Jarena Lee, I hereby withdraw my membership." Richard Allen was one of the founders of the AME Church who left the Methodist Episcopal Church due to racial discrimination. Jarena Lee was one of the first women preachers in the AME Church who the denomination refused to authorize initially.

There, I told him! Of course, Rev. lied to the congregation telling them I quit ministry all together and dropped out of school. Abusers have to control the narrative. Not one member of Allen Chapel called me to verify his account or check on my well-being. It was time to move on after making a clean break from the AME Church. Within a week, my symptoms began to clear and my overall health improved. The shackles were off when I returned to seminary for my final year. My spirit was unbound, but I was mad as hell.

Next, came the hard part: telling my parents. I had shielded them from my struggles within the church as I did not want to dissuade them from joining one day. They shared the same faith, but did not belong to a congregation for their own individual reasons. Exposing their children to religious training remained important for them, nonetheless.

My mother called me every Sunday at seven o'clock while I was away in school. Anyone who knew me well, knew not to bother me during this hour as did her acquaintances. Each conversation started the same with inquiries into our respective well-being, followed by a summary of our week and updates on friends, family, and the dog. Not once had I shared my pastor's obstruction of ordination and the resulting pain. I reserved that for my classmates who were all too familiar with such occurrences.

The previous semester, I happened to be taking homiletics from the professor who was also an ordained elder in the AME Church. Each member of the class had the opportunity to preach brief sermons weekly.

The week following Annual Conference, I preached about my sense of betrayal in my own household of faith. Telling my story openly for the first time was cathartic, but to the displeasure of my instructor and some classmates. They took offense at my airing of the Black church's dirty laundry as if outsiders were unaware. This escalated the enmity between my professor and me.

One day the following week, a fellow seminarian who was a member of a congregation in the Washington Annual Conference approached me in the hallway. She said, "don't go around complaining about being discriminated against if you don't even show up for conference." Every fiber of my flesh was inclined to beat her senseless only to be restrained by the Holy Spirit within. I had never experienced fiery rage like that before. It was only then that I realized these hands ain't saved. I retreated off campus to my apartment immediately and wrote the Dean of Students a letter describing the encounter and its effect. There was no way I could promise the same level of self-control should such a thing happen again.

Professor of psychology and women's studies, Phyllis Chesler, stated:

> While women may not act aggressively in the same way that men do, studies confirm that girls and women are aggressive, often in indirect ways, and mainly toward each other. They judge each other harshly, in life and on juries, hold grudges, gossip about, exclude and disconnect from other women. Women envy and compete against each other, not against men. Women tend to deny that this is true, even to themselves. Since women depend upon each other for emotional intimacy and bonding, the power to form cliques and to shun each other functions to enforce female conformity and to discourage female independence and psychological growth.[25]

Such is definitely true in the church. Women are the overwhelming majority of Black church members, yet do not show much solidarity. For this reason, most in ministry serve at the pleasure of men. It is quite common to hear female preachers praise the vilest male minister profusely only to curry favor for herself. There is no rational reason for

Black women not to be in control of the organization or at a minimum end our own oppression.

Now that the cat was out of the bag, I could be open with my family. It came out once my mother and I completed our opening routine the following Sunday.

"What's new?" she asked.

"I'm thinking about leaving the church" I replied and went on to describe how hostile the environment had become due to Rev.'s bullying and harassment.

Without missing a beat, she said "I'm not surprised. You see, I know that motherfucker's no good. I was wondering about you." I curled up on my cream leather sofa, holding a throw pillow against my abdomen with one hand and the phone nestled to my ear with the other. Mom had already done her reconnaissance on the old man with whom her baby girl had been spending so much time. Her words were at once humiliating and reassuring.

Hilda Brown is far more street smart than her nerdy and often aloof youngest child. She was born in poverty in Rocky Mount, North Carolina, relocated to Washington, DC in the first grade, orphaned at age eight, and raised subsequently in New York City. Suffice to say she had a rough, unstable upbringing. The luxury of being sheltered from anything was never afforded to her. Therefore, she sought to protect her children from how cruel the world can be. Her childhood best friend worked for many years at the Government Printing Office from which Rev. retired. She filled Mom in on his character and shenanigans from the beginning, but my mother never breathed a word of it to me.

Mom's anger was palpable. You simply do not mess with her children lest she become a ferocious mama bear. She did not trust daycare and remained a stay-at-home parent until I entered school all day. She then volunteered at my elementary school and eventually became a para professional aide there. Mom is as protective of the children in her orbit as she is her own.

"So, what do you want me to do about it?" she inquired. It felt noble to say "leave him to God," but I would not have been mad to hear his rotting remains had been found in a dumpster. Had I said the word, I am sure she would have had him dealt with. However, she never said another word about him following this conversation. We went on to discuss how I would be able to afford the remainder of my studies. Never had I disclosed the meager sum the church contributed to my education.

My parents supported me financially for the remainder of my studies, despite my father having just retired. They also provided a safe place for me to land after graduation until I regained my financial footing. Not once, to this day, have they made me eat crow. They must have an off-shore account hidden somewhere because they have always been able to pull money out of a hat to meet their children's needs. (I would like to think their coffers are more like the widow at Zarephath). Years later, I shared that I might be laid off due to the pending sale of the consulting firm where I was employed at the time. My mother responded with all bravado, "How much do they want for it?" Such graciousness I have never found in the church or elsewhere. God provided for me every step along the way, just not in the ways I expected.

It was only a matter of time that I would leave organized religion being independent by upbringing and a cynic by nature. The fact that my parents do not claim membership in a congregation or identify with a denomination provided me with the liberty not to attach too much to an organization. My father also encouraged intellectual freedom by engaging my siblings and me in debates about just about everything under the sun when we were growing up. Whether I leveraged my disposition appropriately is another question. When I eventually moved from membership in the AME Church to the United Methodist Church, my level of attachment declined further.

While I had great respect for each organization, membership by no means meant that I subscribed to all their teachings. Our ultimate partings unleashed theological leanings that I dared not reveal before. Some people act like severing organizational ties is an act of apostasy. A member of Asbury scolded me surmising that I was jeopardizing my salvation by leaving. I told him there is more of God outside the organizational boundaries than inside them and I would take my chances on the former.

Imagine being born and dying in the same house without ever moving to pursue one's own life. That is what happens to some who are introduced to Christendom in childhood and attend church by rote for the rest of their lives without ever deciding for themselves. Such a person would never discern their preferences for expressing faith, develop their mind sufficiently to love God fully, or be able to manage their own spiritual affairs.

Recall the movie *Step Brothers* starring Will Ferrell and John C. Reilly as two middle-aged man-children whose parents marry. They were forced to live together as siblings as neither was self-sufficient nor had ever left the nest. Both characters had infantile sensibilities and habits to match. True to form, the story is a series of one madcap scene after another in which neither is able to function as a full-fledged adult. It is a hilarious scenario unless you have a similar co-dependent in your life.

This is quite an exaggeration, but reflects the same situation in which many traditional churchgoers find themselves. Individuation is the process whereby people detach themselves from their family and communities of origin to establish their own identity and values. Famed psychiatrist Carl Jung described it as a necessary step in human development toward self-actualization. Only an individuated person can maintain values in all seasons and situations. Otherwise, they merely live out the life and truth of others.

Just as individuals must mature physically and psychologically, full faith requires significant spiritual development beyond what families of origin and organized religion can provide. Doing so does not require every believer to pursue formal theological training. But by waiting to be spoon-fed simple instructions on how to live and what to think, underdeveloped parishioners overextend their pastors, mindlessly endure all manner of religious foolishness, and deprive themselves of the opportunity to contribute their best to the fold and the world. It is dangerous to stake one's eternal destiny on the possibility that someone else might have gotten it wrong.

Church is not about finding consensus or strengthening familial and social bonds. Jesus said:

Do not suppose that I have come to bring peace to the earth.
I did not come to bring peace, but a sword. For I have come
to turn
a man against his father,
a daughter against her mother,
a daughter-in-law against her mother-in-law—
a [person]'s enemies will be the members of [their] own household.

Carrying one's cross means to prefer Christ above all else. The willingness to endure enmity with loved ones is paramount. Taking a theological position or preserving church membership to maintain unity with one's kin is not biblical, but rather worldly.

It is equally as perilous for the church to deliberately under-develop believers to maintain an unhealthy sense of dependence on the institution. Low-functioning believers—some of whom are ministers—are often high-functioning in other areas of life. Conversely, some believers of modest educational and professional attainment have a well-cultivated spirituality. Traditional religion breeds a simplistic, childlike trust without attaining consciousness of what God requires of them individually or in community. The pastor should never be the only member of the congregation who can lead prayer, visit the sick, console the bereaved, teach, and even preach. Christianity is a priesthood of all believers. A body of mature members will be able to perform most of the duties usually reserved for a full-time pastor. Administrative and counseling duties can be outsourced to a competent therapist or business professional.

Few institutions are willing to entertain contrary notions with the potential to drive business away. When they do, it is usually for the purpose of refuting the idea rather than examining it on its own merit. Just as hospitals discharge its patients and schools graduate its students, churches need some form of closure to its spiritual formation process lest members die on the vine from being overfed yet malnourished. Bloated rolls are more a reflection of a failure to launch than production of disciples.

If a believer cannot provide an account of their faith without leaning on the statements of their pastor or denomination, then it is shaky. The gospel would not have stood the test of time were it vulnerable to human inquiry. *For the message of the cross is foolishness to those who are perishing, but to us who are being saved it is the power of God.*

According to Carl Jung:

> The seat of faith, however, is not consciousness but spontaneous religious experience, which brings the individual's faith into immediate relation with God. Here we must ask: Have I any religious experience and immediate relation to God, and hence that certainty which will keep me, as an individual, from dissolving in the crowd?[26]

The church must trust God enough to let the Spirit flourish and its members go into the world exercising their faith freely.

The pain of separating from organized religion brought my formal liturgies and forced attendance to an abrupt end. It also led me to further cultivate personal rituals and perform honest soul work. No more did structured petitions to the divine preoccupy my mind. When I prayed, there were often sweat, snot, and tears as I told God how I really felt about Him and His people. This took a great degree of courage and vulnerability. We discussed things I could not bring myself to acknowledge previously. And I listened more than I spoke.

Being honest required concurrent action. I could not continue to pretend the communities in which I found myself were, for me, the body of Christ. They took no interest in God's interest in me. In the spirit of Ta-Nehisi Coates, "You won't enroll me in this lie. You won't make me part of it."[27] I once volunteered to uphold the falsehoods of Christendom, but no longer have any motivation to do so. However, my relationship with God remains the one immutable constant in my journey.

9

INSTITUTIONAL ILLUSIONS

There is none so blind as those who will not see.

Matthew Henry

It is not an unreasonable expectation to find love in God's house. I have made some good friends and had some warm encounters with individuals in church. But I can say I still have not found that deep, benevolent, abiding love that characterizes God in a community as a whole. I John 4:7 says, *Beloved, let us love one another, for love is from God; and everyone who loves is born of God and knows God.*

This begs the question of whether most church people really know God or just like dropping God's name. Faking it is easy and often expedient to filling the pews and separating people from their money. The verse following the above passage presents the other side of the proposition. *The one who does not love does not know God, for God is love.* It is as simple as that. Jesus said himself: *So then, you will know them by their fruits.*

Ironically, I have experienced some of the most loving encounters with strangers and those who are not overtly religious. That is not unlike Jesus' experience with the religious establishment of his day. The Samaritan woman at the well in the fourth chapter of the Gospel of John had been victimized and marginalized, yet was very receptive and accommodating to Jesus. By no coincidence, she became a great evangelist—even ahead of the original twelve disciples who did not comprehend her encounter with him. *He came to His own, and those who were His own did not receive Him. But as many as received Him, to them He gave the right to become children of God.*

Indifference can have a stronger effect psychologically than either love or hate. In the same manner, I have experienced multiple periods of prolonged unemployment while my fellow believers peered voyeuristically without offering any assistance. The greatest surprise was not false friends, but those who showed they cared deeply about my well-being unbeknownst to me.

I got laid off twice within two years following the market crash of 2008. The second time I started my own consulting practice to seize the momentum created in the healthcare market following the passage of the Affordable Care Act. Demand was high initially as organizations needed insight on meeting the law's requirements and leverage funding opportunities. Then everybody got in on the game. I learned quickly that the contract does not always go to the smartest or most qualified. Those with political connections used them to get into coveted spaces where they might not have had the expertise. I made lots of money while fully-engaged. However, my income fluctuated dramatically as I navigated natural business cycles.

I came close to foreclosure, having my car repossessed, and even not knowing how my basic needs would be met at times. By the grace of God, there were people in my life for whom that was unacceptable and they moved to prevent unfavorable outcomes however they could. It all added up and revealed who was in which category. Members of various churches have shared stories with me of departing after not receiving more than thoughts and prayers or some other form of nonchalance following the loss of a loved one or another personal crisis. Even in my challenges with pursuing ministry, church folks could not have cared less about the outcome. Meanwhile, my friends whose church attendance is as spotty as mine remain the ones who breathe new life in me to pursue God's will.

Boldness is another intrinsic quality of the church. That is good because I walk in that power despite my petite physical stature. There are three things I find particularly offensive when weak: a man, a cocktail, and a believer. We all have flaws, but habitual excuse-making while claiming the power of the Holy Spirit makes me want to holler like Marvin Gaye. From the failure to discern blatant offenses, to the fear of responding when things are amiss and the refusal to love universally. Believers have collectively developed a crippling lethargy that allows outsiders to look inside the church with revulsion.

They say "he's just a man" or "we all make mistakes." Yes, all human beings are fallible. However, reducing our moral standards to the lowest common denominator blasphemes the Holy Spirit. *[We] can do all things through Christ who strengthens [us].* Prior to his ascension, Jesus promised we would receive power when the Holy Spirit comes to us. The same spirit was prophesied by Joel to fall on not just preachers, but all flesh. With that power comes authority.

> *For the grace of God has appeared, bringing salvation to all [people], instructing us to deny ungodliness and worldly desires and to live sensibly, righteously, and in a godly manner in the present age, looking for the blessed hope and the appearing of the glory of our great God and Savior, Christ Jesus, who gave Himself for us to redeem us from every lawless deed, and to purify for Himself a people for His own possession, eager for good deeds. These things speak and exhort, and rebuke with all authority. No one is to disregard you.*

It was downright embarrassing to witness some portions of my hometown under siege by drug activity and violence in the late 1980s through the 1990s. Although I was away at school for most of that period, I was not scared of walking the streets and going about life while at home. Some of my acquaintances who were in the underground economy actually kept a close eye to ensure my safety. Besides that, I knew who walked with me. As is typical of urban neighborhoods, churches were on almost every corner singing about the power in the blood. Yet, nobody was afraid of them and they dared not confront the danger outside their doors. Meanwhile, the brothers of the Nation of Islam patrolled some of the most violent neighborhoods to keep them safe.

If I had a dollar for every time someone said "Just who in the hell does she think she is?", I would be a Republican. I have never been good at playing the shrinking violet. Most of what passes for God's will does not require a keen sense of discernment to detect. However, taking the risk of addressing sin is precisely what the gospel demands. *If your right eye causes you to stumble, gouge it out and throw it away. It is better for you to lose one part of your body than for your whole body to be thrown into hell.*

Just like the ushers are responsible for welcoming people, churches need a ministry dedicated to kicking people out. (Eureka! That just might be my assignment). Saints have been endowed with the authority to assess the quality of those within the boundaries of the church. *What business is it of mine to judge those outside the church? Are you not to judge those inside? God will judge those outside. Expel the wicked person from among you.*

Many people have little problem giving expression to the movement of the Spirit during worship. Let that same movement reveal something amiss and they show themselves to be spiritual weaklings. "I'll go pray on it" they say reflexively. In other words, they are going to stick their heads in the proverbial sand. Times like these are when the devil does his happy dance. God is calling you to get off your rump. *For God hast not given us the spirit of fear; but of power, and of love, and of a sound mind.*

In the same manner, large religious gatherings were common to cycle in and out of Atlanta with it being a major hub in the Bible Belt. Every summer, one prominent speaker after another would rent large arenas for their signature conference. These were all-day and sometimes multi-day affairs. People came from across the sprawling Atlanta metropolitan area and beyond. The cost of attending was beyond my budget. Some charged no admission, but leaned hard on your pockets with an appeal to contribute at the end.

One of my classmates was deliberating about whether or not she should attend, but eventually answered her own question. She realized that with thousands, and sometimes tens of thousands, of attendees, power should be emanating from them. The lack thereof was her observation as a former supporter of said conferences. Most people we knew who attended left with a temporary emotional high, but unchanged.

Feebleness in the kingdom is about as worthless as a watered-down drink. God apparently agrees with me. Jesus did not turn the wine into water, did he? One of my favorite biblical phrases is when God tells Job repeatedly to *gird up your loins like a man* as Job wavered in faith. Believers need to man-up to conquer everything that is an impediment to the redemptive works of God in themselves, their communities, and the world. That is the essence of faith. *Even so faith, if it has no works, is dead.*

Richard Pryor told a joke about a man caught in the act of adultery. The man jumped off his lover and pleaded with his wife. "Who you gonna believe, me or your lying eyes?" That is exactly how I felt as everything I believed about the church clashed with my personal experience with the institution.

Cognitive dissonance occurs when a person holds contradictory beliefs, ideas, or values, and is typically experienced as psychological stress when they participate in an action that goes against one or more of them.[28] The first-generation church struggled to reconcile the victorious Jesus' promise of abundant life while they were being deprived of property, persecuted, and executed for merely following him. My struggle was mostly existential, but likewise crisis-inducing.

Religious organizations can seem like such godless places at times and the faith walk can be quite lonely despite being surrounded by people. However, restoration is not beyond the reach of God. The problem is most churches do not equip members for the time of trial or respect the process itself. I clutched my pearls the first time I read *You will be hated by all because of my name.* In contrast, my early Christian education made it seem like the gospel was akin to a Dale Carnegie course. Adhering to the teachings of Jesus will do more to lose friends and alienate people than vice versa. More people fall away from the false certainty of religious doctrine than from the overwhelmingly otherness of the unsearchable God. Even clergy wrestle with their faith privately, without a safe space to do so openly.

Jesus' first cousin, John the Baptist, jumped with joy in the womb whenever their mothers came together during pregnancy. Yet, while he was imprisoned for preaching the Gospel and awaiting execution, *he sent a message to Jesus. "Are you the one who is to come, or should we expect someone else?"* If someone so intimately acquainted with our Savior experienced such angst, how much more will it be for those of us far removed from his earthly presence? Like many believers before me, I had to decide whether God was indeed reconciling the world unto Himself by the perfecting work of the Holy Spirit or this whole church thing was a sham.

Being part of such a learned gentry, my original vision was to pursue doctoral theological studies and an academic career. Ordination was merely an accessory. A significant portion of my seminary professors were ordained in their respective sects, but only a small subset was active in them. That seemed like an acceptable proposition to me.

In the meantime, I was going crazy trying to pretend my eyes were deceiving me and faith could move the monumental black ball Rev. had placed me behind. All the conflicting notions were pushing me to the edge. The stress of feeling I could not leave the denomination in which both my faith was born and social location grounded was juxtaposed against knowing I must release my identification with the institution that was oppressing me.

One would think the primary questions to me as a candidate for ministry would have been about my salvation or the call itself. Did it originate from God or a fit of psychosis? I have had a lot of psychotherapy and am off the charts with neuroses. The luxury of being detached from reality that psychosis provides would have been a welcome relief. Never have I been examined about either my salvation or calling outside of a seminary setting.

Later readings describing God's nature and interactions with humanity confirmed the validity of my call. I will not belabor the matter here because words would fail. Scripture even confirmed the elements of my vision and the sound of God's voice. The greatest evidence was that it provoked me to reorient my life in pursuit of my calling. Had God not given me such a clear and empowering revelation, I would have fallen away at the manifold signs of trouble.

William Myers wrote a pair of companion books that further confirmed this was not a figment of my imagination: *The Irresistible Urge to Preach* and *God's Yes Was Louder Than My No*. They are a collection of call stories from prominent ministers of the gospel. The similarities to mine revealed the stunning consistency of the divine. God bless whoever turned me onto them. God bless even more the scofflaw who borrowed my books and never returned them. May their fire never grow cold.

While still in seminary, I had the pleasure of meeting theologian James Cone, who happened to be an ordained minister in the AME Church. He had just delivered a lecture at the Washington National Cathedral and was signing books for his adoring public. When my turn came, I asked what the role of the theologian was among such esteemed Black folks. He replied, "there is none; they just like to parade you around as if you are relevant to them."

Around the same time, I had the pleasure of meeting individually with womanist theologian Jacqueline Grant at her office at the Interdenominational Theological Center in Atlanta. Reading her book *White Women's Christ and Black Women's Jesus* before attending seminary awakened my womanist sensibilities. She indulged me as I pondered a future following the trail she blazed and pretty much told me the same thing. That essentially sealed it for me and I left the organization a few months later.

When I entered the ordination process in the United Methodist church years later, similar issues arose. First, they knew I was a single woman with a mortgage and a boatload of student loans that their salaries could not cover. Likewise, the Roman Catholic Church does not allow priests to marry. It has nothing to do with theology, but everything to do with money. Supporting single men is far less costly than providing for families. I was also pretty clear at this point that I did not see myself pastoring a church. They expressed a problem with my non-institutional career aspirations despite having a pipeline of talented, yet underemployed, clergy members. Why could ministers not keep a secular day job, especially if the organization could not afford to support them?

Nowhere in the New Testament is the concept of entitlement for church leaders promoted. No, the ox should not be muzzled, but neither shall it be overindulged. Torah required eleven of the twelve Israelite tribes to give a tenth of their material benefits to support the Levites, the tribe responsible for the priestly and ritualistic duties of the cult. Jesus' finished work on the cross satisfied the ritualistic requirements of the law permanently. Consequently, all believers gained direct access to God and the priests lost their jobs.

Tithing is one of the hardest sells within the church today. On the surface, it doesn't seem unreasonable for believers to give God a ten percent cut of their income. The average American spends a significant portion of their money frivolously anyway. Ten percent is not a real sacrifice. Then why is it so hard to get people to come up off their cash? The reason tithing is so hard to sell is because it is not necessary.

The New Testament doesn't speak much of tithing. Jesus labeled it one of the lesser parts of the law. *Woe to you, teachers of the law and Pharisees, you hypocrites! You give a tenth of your spices—mint, dill and cumin. But you have neglected the more important matters of the law— justice, mercy and faithfulness. You should have practiced the latter, without neglecting the former.* To hear the church tell it today, your faith is weak if you are not giving legalistically.

The law is not a compelling argument for much of anything juxtaposed with the grace offered by the gospel. The most often quoted verse before the collection is Malachi 3:8-10.

> *Will a man rob God? Yet ye have robbed me. But ye say, Wherein have we robbed thee? In tithes and offerings. Ye are cursed with a curse: for ye have robbed me, even this whole nation. Bring ye all the tithes into the storehouse, that there may be meat in mine house, and prove me now herewith, saith the Lord of hosts, if I will not open you the windows of heaven, and pour you out a blessing, that there shall not be room enough to receive it.*

In all my years of compulsive churchgoing, I have never heard this text preached right. Go back and read it yourself in context. Neither advanced exegetical techniques nor knowledge of the Hebrew language is necessary to comprehend. Simply read the opening of the preceding chapter. God directed this rebuke at the priests who were withholding proper sacrifices from God. The people were giving right. The priests were the ones stealing by not using the gifts for their intended purpose. People today watch passively knowing their contributions are not being used to advance the kingdom, yet continue to invest in unfruitful ministries.

Jesus did not come to create an investment club whereby tithes and offerings provide returns to elevate one's economic standing. The abundant life Jesus promised is about transcendent power beyond the things of this world. Adherents to the prosperity gospel think if they spring for a jet, palatial estate, and premium automobile for their spiritual leader, then they should be good for a scaled-down version of such excess. Most of them are as broke as the Ten Commandments. People with no more than a bus pass should not be buying Bentleys for others. Jesus rode a donkey. Trickledown economics do not work and neither does trickledown stewardship. The most hardened hustlers blush as they watch preachers charm and coerce parishioners to hand over money to which they have no right or meaningful purpose.

The two main guidelines for giving in the New Testament fly in the face of tithing. On the left is 2 Corinthians 9:7. *Each of you should give what you have decided in your heart to give, not reluctantly or under compulsion, for God loves a cheerful giver.* God does not need your money to accomplish redemption. The show will go on with or without your offerings.

Before you get slap happy, perfection of faith is on the right. *Jesus said "If you want to be perfect, go, sell your possessions and give to the poor, and you will have treasure in heaven. Then come, follow me."* Notice Jesus did not say give to the religious establishment, but rather to the poor. The first-generation church shared all their possessions in common. Today's "Evanpublicans" would have no part of that. Christendom has bought wholeheartedly into the individualism of capitalism, which is antithetical to the gospel. Rare is the congregation that allocates a large proportion of its annual budget to charity as opposed to institutional maintenance.

Churches would be empty if any form of socialism became the standard. That is why pastors do not interpret Malachi properly. Parishioners do not extend themselves to do so either. Instead, both sides collude to accept a compromised standard for giving. Give the church a cut and you can do whatever the hell you want. This is no different from the Catholic Church selling indulgences centuries ago. Today's methods are just not as blatant. In exchange, we do not ensure the treasury is going toward real kingdom building. That too would require more of us than is comfortable.

We do not even share the same elements during the Eucharist. Churches have abandoned the communal partaking of the bread and cup in the same manner it has adopted the individualistic values of Western culture. Prepackaged synthetic wafers and a shot of diluted grape drink have replaced the loaf and chalice. What is really being celebrated?

I Peter 2:9 declares all believers to be priests. *But you are a chosen people, a royal priesthood, a holy nation, God's special possession, that you may declare the praises of him who called you out of darkness into his wonderful light.* If this is true, we all should get a cut of the collection plate as a member of the new Levitical tribe. Go to your pastor and demand your share of the take. Let me know how that works out for you.

I approached Rev. at the conclusion of my first year of seminary to ask him if the church would pay my rent for June since the first payday of my summer job was not scheduled until later in the month. You would have thought I asked him for a kidney instead of a few hundred dollars. Rev. responded that the church would give me half. I responded that I hoped only to get halfway put out. This was not an extraordinary request given the congregation had an annual budget in excess of a million dollars and never ever compensated me for services rendered. As always, my parents came to the rescue.

Rev. took it personally that someone was infringing on his purse. He had devoted officers who were more loyal to the pastor than to God. They would skim a portion of the cash contributions for Rev. prior to counting the collection. This was despite the fact that he drew a generous compensation package. It was not unusual for a member of the community to approach him when facing hardship. I have seen him peel bills from a large bankroll in his pocket to assist less out of good will than to solidify his position. Soon after Allen Chapel gave me five-hundred dollars as I departed for seminary, they bought Rev. a brand-new S-Class Mercedes Benz.

The angriest I have ever seen Rev. was when we failed to take up a collection during a service held in his absence. It was an evening program, maybe a choir's anniversary or something similar. He had a conflicting commitment at another church. The junior officers in charge of the order of the day got caught up in the excitement of worship and concluded the service after we collectively came down from it. Rev. flew into a rage the next day when he learned of this missed opportunity to rake in cash. He wanted to hear nothing of what a good time we had in the Lord. If the service did not generate revenue, he did not see its value. The offertory hymn might as well have been "Bitch Better Have My Money."

The Catholic and most Protestant churches dispute all believers have equal access to God in the face of overwhelming scriptural evidence to the contrary. Jesus was a threat to the Judaic priests of his day since his perfect sacrifice abolished their jobs. Because He lives forever, Jesus holds His priesthood perpetually. The institutional church wants us to believe that we still need a priestly system—the clergy—as an intermediary and demands fees to intercede on our behalf. Go ahead and throw the whole book of Hebrews out the stained-glass windows.

The strange part is that the answers are within the grasp of anyone willing to engage Scripture with an open heart and mind. If preachers would concern themselves with ministering to the soul before dipping into congregants' pockets, they would never want for anything. We have been offered something better by way of the new covenant. Rather, the church prefers to forsake its spiritual birthright by reverting to a form of neo-Judaism. God changed the game with Jesus Christ, but the institution wants it to remain the same.

About three months after my final encounter with Rev., I stood up at work while wearing a blush-colored wool pantsuit. Blood gushed like a dam had broken between my legs. The light color made it impossible to conceal. I had to act quickly before anyone noticed. It seemed that running into Rev. triggered me and my body responded in-kind. This was the last straw. I could no longer stand the breakthrough bleeding that had been tormenting me for the decade I had been pursuing ministry. Physicians failed to diagnose the source or bring it to an end over the years.

My stained clothing made me want to reach inside and rip my uterus out my body. I grabbed my belongings and hurried out of the office without explanation. The wet itchy fabric was terribly uncomfortable against the cold December air. As soon as I got in the car for the drive home, I got on the phone with my mother. The time was long overdue for me to visit her gynecologist of almost forty years. It is my nature to want to do things my way. My way was failing me in this case.

John P. George was born in the Caribbean island of Grenada and trained professionally at the Howard University School of Medicine. His office was not in the best neighborhood, not as well-appointed as some of the tony practices I had visited, nor was it the model of efficiency. His schedule was always backlogged and he did not employ the latest technology in electronic health records. That did not stop women from all over the region from flocking to his practice and waiting patiently because he was legendary. During my intake, he simply asked what was going on with me. This was the first time I was offered the opportunity to speak uninterruptedly about my experiences and medical history for an extended amount of time.

He nailed my diagnosis without ever touching my body.

"Sounds like adenomyosis," a rare condition in which endometrial tissue lining the uterus invades the inner uterine wall. Pelvic pain, heavy periods, and noncyclic bleeding often result.

I responded "you treated my mother for that long ago, as well as two of my sisters in recent years for other conditions."

"Who is your mother?" he inquired.

When I said her name, he looked at my face, unleashed a broad smile, and gave me the biggest hug. Only then did he notice the strong resemblance. Dr. George chastised me for not coming to him sooner. I told him I was trying to find my own way through life. He said his history with my family is exactly why I should have come to him first. He never lied. That man is a pussy savant.

Subsequent diagnostic tests and imaging confirmed his hypothesis. All other doctors simply heard my symptoms and assumed one of the more common conditions among Black women—fibroids, ovarian cyst, or endometriosis—was the cause. When those tests were negative, they stopped searching. The previous physicians were efficient in their operations, but not terribly effective in their treatment. Rushing me through the time allotted for my appointment wasted a lot of resources used to speculate. Had they listened to me intently, I could have been cured much sooner.

Dr. George described my options during my follow-up visit. I told him he only had one chance to cut me and opted for a total hysterectomy (removal of the uterus, with fallopian tubes and ovaries intact). When he asked when I wanted to do it, I asked for his earliest availability. We scheduled the surgery for a few weeks out and the rest is history. The procedure itself was uneventful. My mother attended to me during my admission, recovery, and discharge as if she were part of the medical staff. Dr. George provided her with constant updates, HIPAA be damned. He even offered to make a home call if any complications arose.

Never have I been in more loving hands in a clinical environment than in the care of Dr. George. I joined his cult following and went into an existential crisis. His non-institutional practice of medicine went against everything I espoused as a management consultant. My own poison was not palatable as a patient. Now I realize efficiency, consistency, and technology should never be prioritized over love and mindfulness. Mass produced, assembly-line medicine no longer appealed to me and I now only opt for highly personalized practices. And so it is with ministries.

Chronic insomnia set in and limited my ability to function. I was only able to powernap while in the hospital and could not sleep more than a couple hours at a time for seven months thereafter. Tests of my endocrine system were negative for diabetes and menopause. A reproductive psychiatrist treated me to help stabilize my mood and biochemical balance. Her typical caseload includes women who have experienced rape, miscarriages, domestic violence, or major hormonal disruptions. Two-and-a-half years under her care was a great privilege as she does not advertise, accept insurance, or take just anyone as a patient.

My experience with the church arose while sharing my personal history. I mentioned it flippantly, but she recognized the traumatic effect immediately. We worked together to unpack the events I had been unable to process, leading me to the healing I was not able to find elsewhere. God is good because I would have never selected a non-Christian for such a sensitive task left to my own devices. She was Jewish, but well-acquainted with the ways of organized religion in general. That actually turned out to be the greatest benefit because she had no motive to steer me back to the environment that proved not to be healthy for me.

10

AN INCONVENIENT TRUTH

The only difference between a rut and a grave is in their dimensions.

Ellen Glasglow

From the time I accepted my calling until this writing, it never dawned on me that ordained ministry might not be the most suitable path. A licensed preacher from our congregation was a candidate for ordination during the first Annual Conference following my initial sermon. However, the Board of Examiners did not recommend him. Deals were made under the table and he was lined up with a robe among ministers to be consecrated at the Annual Conference. That same year, he was appointed to a good-sized church in the deep South. Within a few years, their building fund was gone and so was he.

It was not so far-fetched that I could be ordained through some backdoor wheeling and dealing. Such happens all the time. But why was my name never presented to the Board of Examiners? Why was the church not formally informed my candidacy was being held in abeyance? Each congregational report indicated I was on track to be ordained according to the customary schedule. Those who attended local denominational conferences knew otherwise, but did nothing.

My challenges in pursuing ordained ministry had nothing to do with my character, intelligence, or spirituality. The AME Church was supposed to be as good as it gets for Black women in ministry. The denomination has a written policy against sexual harassment that I learned almost never gets enforced. I would speak dismissively to my sisters in other denominations. "That's how it goes; you're Baptist. What do you expect as a Pentecostal?" and so on. The sad state of affairs is that while ahead of its peer institutions, the AME church sets a very low bar.

St. Philip, the AME congregation with which I affiliated while away in seminary, was a combination of Ward Memorial, the church of my youth, and Allen Chapel. Services had a traditional style. The congregation was vibrant and on the verge of becoming a megachurch. The pastor was just as senior and influential as Rev. If anyone could fix this for me, he could. I told him the whole sordid story after my chances were dashed back home. His face reddened as he listened.

The pastor pounded his fist on his large, stately desk exclaiming, "Dammit, I hate when they do this!" He then stormed out of his office for a few minutes and returned emitting a long sigh. He sat on the same side of the desk as me, held my hand, and leaned in. I sat motionless while he collected his thoughts.

"This is what we're going to do. Preach another initial sermon here in Atlanta and start the ordination process from square one under me."

I said "How can I preach an initial sermon twice? Pretending my previous experience never happened is unacceptable."

He replied with resignation, "I know, but that's the best I can offer."

"I appreciate what you're trying to do, but I can't."

"I just don't want you to return home emptyhanded after all you've done."

"Remaining in Atlanta after graduation to complete the process is out of the question and I'm not continuing it in DC."

We departed with a mutual embrace and teary eyes.

I had no choice except to leave the AME Church. The church had broken faith with me for all practical purposes. People had been telling me countless times that I needed to leave the denomination, but I was waiting to hear it from Mount Sinai. One loses perspective the longer one remains in an institution or the more vested one is in it. The obvious became my only option.

By the grace of my classmates, I did receive invitations to preach and teach at churches around the Atlanta metropolitan area. Some of them knew of my situation and did so out of pity. Most others did not and did so out of recognition of my gifts and preparation. Some were Black. Some were white. I was always welcomed warmly. Not one of them was of my own denomination. I was never invited to preach at an AME Church during seminary nor any time thereafter. An officer at Ward Memorial approached me during one of my more recent visits saying the church had been wanting to invite me to speak, but had no way of contacting me. I said, "Dude, we are Facebook friends." Crickets.

Other opportunities presented themselves for me to be ordained. A friend of a friend who was an AME pastor offered to let me transfer my membership to his church several states away. My absence from church and conferences could be excused by being away attending seminary at the time. I gave the offer serious consideration, but ultimately declined. Although expedient, the same people and dynamics would await me after graduation. He breathed a sigh of relief as ordaining me would have had serious political ramifications for him.

The Bishop in Residence at Candler offered to have me ordained in the United Methodist Church after learning of my travails in the AME Church. His only caveat was that I had to get married as soon as possible because they do not like single ministers down South. As flattered as I was at his generosity, I refused to play games with my life like that. I had no serious suitors and dared not yoke up with another minister in the same predicament.

That offer revealed why there is such a mad rush of seminarians getting married as they near ordination or ministers being considered for appointments to pastoral positions. Many of the pairings are as awkward as the circumstances leading up to them. An older female minister warned me never to consent to an arranged marriage in the church. She advised that any man in the Black church who has to be forced to get married is either a whoremonger, homosexual, or an unsuitable choice for me for some other undisclosed reason. I later learned of plenty of cases of strange unions at the behest of the church without regard to the well-being of the unsuspecting spouses.

I knew a pastor who was married to a woman for over twenty years despite the fact he was gay. She cherished her role as first lady with the incumbent big hats, prime seating, and constant recognition. Although they shared a strong sense of partnership, their lack of chemistry was evident. Church officials were well aware of his homosexuality, but did not object because he employed a beard. His sexual orientation was never a problem until he sought a powerful position within the denomination. A competitor threatened to reveal his secret, thus forcing him to withdraw his candidacy. He often ended his sermons singing:

> Shackled by a heavy burden,
> 'Neath a load of guilt and shame…

The truth was revealed when he died of AIDS. His wife died many years later following a lengthy, but unspecified, illness.

When I left seminary, my plan was to return home to my day job and put the religious training behind me. At times I was able to maintain a sense of oblivion about my ministry and lead what passed for a normal life. Then seasons of rumination over what I could have done differently to change the outcome would emerge. I did not attend church much at all, but something deep within compelled me to visit different ones periodically. Seemed like I could not go long without being in community with fellow believers. The pull of corporate worship and fellowship with the saints was magnetic. The more I resisted, the greater the pull. But I kept my calling under my hat.

Returning to DC without being ordained was one of the most abject moments of failure I ever experienced. Just four years prior, I stood before several hundred people on a Sunday evening and proclaimed my entry into the profession of ministry as I preached my initial sermon. It was not the greatest oratorical presentation of my lifetime, but it represented the greatest leap of faith. As a classic overachiever, I strove toward my goals with intensity. I served as President of my elementary school, junior high, and high school graduating classes. Offers of admission were extended by my first choice of undergraduate and graduate schools, as well as seminary. I was also accepted into my preferred Sorority on the first try. Ordination was supposed to be a slam dunk.

Almost a year after my initial sermon, I put my all on the altar by quitting my job and moving to Atlanta sight-unseen to pursue theological training. That size faith should have moved the mountain before me.

When met with the initial resistance from Rev., I took rejection in the manner of the character Strangé from the movie *Boomerang*. Nobody was supposed to turn me down, especially when I had attained so many greater things already.

Everything seemed to go wrong from my first weekend in Atlanta, but I rebounded each time. Before classes even began, I cut clear through my left hand between my thumb and forefinger with a knife while chopping vegetables for dinner. Undeterred, I wrapped the gaping bleeding wound tightly and drove myself to the hospital. The staff at Emory University Medical Center stitched my hand closed and released me in less than an hour.

On the first day of classes, an engine seal broke on my car and leaked newly-changed oil all over the parking garage. The next day, I rode my bicycle five miles to school with my hand still bandaged. Although Atlanta is urban, it does not have sidewalks, let alone bike lanes. Drivers were no respector of this cyclist. A classmate from Iowa, who I had only just met, volunteered not only to give me a ride home at the end of the day, but also to the dealership where my vehicle had been towed. There was no way I would have been a match for evening rush hour traffic in Atlanta on a bicycle. A series of other mishaps occurred over the ensuing three years, without much consequence. Each episode increased my confidence that the ordination conundrum would resolve itself.

As my last semester drew to a close, I saw no cause for celebration. While my classmates were making plans for graduation and beyond, my only plans were to move back to DC and pretend the preceding three years never happened. Although living there was a pleasure, I could not get out of Atlanta fast enough. Returning home made forgetting impossible. Each encounter with a familiar face forced me to admit my failure. It is one thing to fall short privately, but to make such a bold move publicly laid my disappointment bare. These types of things were not supposed to happen to me.

At the end of the summer, one of my Sorors invited me to her house to view the 2000 Summer Olympic games. One of our fraternity brothers gravitated to me and we began to chat. In the midst of our back-and-forth, I discerned something peculiar and asked, "Are you called to preach?" He responded affirmatively, but stated he had no intention on accepting it for another twenty years or so when he retired from his job as an airline pilot. We stole away to a corner where I ministered to him. Onlookers were startled by the intensity of our conversation thinking he was wooing me hard. The host came over after we parted to give me the lowdown on which of our Sorors he had been involved with recently. She was stunned to learn the nature of our interaction as was I. It felt like I had an out of body experience in the middle of a party on a Saturday night. That was one of numerous occasions God reminded me that my calling was still intact.

Meanwhile, my parents were wondering aloud why I "paid all that money not to go to church." Just four years prior, I came home grief-stricken announcing that I had something serious to discuss with them. They waited the news with bated breath. First, they suspected I was pregnant. Breathing a sigh of relief, they looked at each other wondering what else it could be. I was sobbing too hard to get my words together. They started telling me how much they loved me and whatever it was would not change that. Then I finally drew enough breaths to tell them I had been called to ministry. They rolled their eyes simultaneously and sighed. "Just go ahead. Why are you crying with your silly self?" I then got myself together and went on at length about how this was not just another phase and I was as serious as ever.

An elderly neighbor who has known me since birth grew frustrated with seeing my long winding walks with my dog on Sunday mornings. She pulled her Lincoln Continental over and wagged her forefinger shouting "You sure are taking this not going to church thing seriously, aren't you?" Then she whisked away to her house of worship. It was like salt in my wounds, but salt does have therapeutic properties.

The greatest contradiction is that I could have spread my legs in the beginning and avoided all conflict with the church. Barriers to ministry would have been few and church members more comfortable with my lack of critique. Fortunately, the thought never crossed my mind. I took God at God's word. When things did not work out as I thought they would, it drove me into an existential crisis. Publicly, I was cool, calm, and collected. Behind closed doors, I cried, clenched my teeth, and questioned the divine fervently.

My experience is far from uncommon, but forbidden to acknowledge. Seldom have I told anyone about my plight—from the well-churched to unbelievers—than they could recall even worse accounts in a religious setting. People have gone so far as to commit suicide as a result of the distress from being oppressed by organized religion. This led me to wonder less about the perpetrators than those individuals who stand by idly without reforming their respective institutions.

The latter reflection is what led me ultimately to leave Allen Chapel AME Church where I accepted my calling. As I was contemplating, one of the biggest players I used to date told me he moved his wife and daughters from their church after recognizing the pastor's game as the same one he once used to exploit women and advised me to do likewise. Congregations and ecclesiastical systems are more true to the game than to the gospel. When they come into conflict, money, membership, and public image will win. Got a problem with that? Then get to stepping.

Along the way, a few congregational pastor friends reached out to me to feign outrage about my plight. They each promised to use their autonomy to ordain me at their respective churches. I never pressed the issue lest I become prone to compromise. Good thing I did not because in each case they made sexual overtures toward me. I consequently stopped communicating with them.

My first post-seminary pastor submitted my name for ordination in the United Methodist Church after I had been at Asbury for a single year. The Replacement who succeeded him did not see fit to advance my candidacy for no stated reason. Almost a decade later, I entered my own name into the process after sitting around wondering when it would happen. The Replacement humored me by sitting passively like he was not opposing me. The District Superintendent invited me to her office for a preliminary meeting when my candidacy finally advanced beyond Charge Conference. Our conversation was cordial as she too was a Black woman close in age to me. She started reading a litany of doctrinal statements in the form "we believe such and such because we are United Methodists."

I responded that she would never hear me say I believe anything because I am a member of a congregation that is part of a particular denomination. My faith is personal and a result of careful deliberation and conviction. Group think is contrary to my nature. I told her we could stop the process at that point if my positions were a problem. The Chair of the District's Committee on Ordained Ministry invited me to interview a few months later at the recommendation of the District Superintendent.

Before the interview even got under way, the District Superintendent recounted my statement from our previous meeting like the character Stephen played by Samuel L. Jackson in the movie *Django*. She looked subserviently at the white female Chair, who was her subordinate. Then she addressed her as if to say, "This here is an uppity one." I freely admitted that I do not believe in the infallibility of every doctrinal statement of the United Methodist Church. For some positions, there is less biblical support than what a group of people assented to at a given point in time. Doctrine is subject to change.

United Methodists take the founder of Methodism more seriously than he took himself. I attended a United Methodist seminary, but only their candidates for ordination had to take classes on John Wesley's theology. The same discipline to which they wanted me to swear allegiance did not even embrace racial equality until after the civil rights movement advanced the cause. Less than a decade before my birth, the denomination would have required me to assent to their view of Black inferiority.

Well, that was the wrong answer. It was not so much that the United Methodist Church is a bastion of theological purity. I have heard all manner of heresy from ordained clergy among its ranks without institutional consequence. As a matter of fact, a pastor at one of the most prominent Methodist Churches in America—down the street from the White House—stated during Bible study that the whole of Scripture was composed of allegorical myths and none of it was to be taken literally. Not one person in the room blinked. I interjected that if Christ did not rise, our faith is in vain and the church needs to go out of business. No one said a word.

One of the most attractive attributes of the denomination for me was its supposed regard for intellectual freedom. My divergence was not over anything fundamental to Christianity. I can recite the Apostle's Creed, which captures the essentials of the faith, with complete agreement.

Their slogan "Open Hearts, Open Doors, Open Minds" apparently just makes for nice bumper stickers.

This encounter was more so about my refusal to respect church leaders' authority than a matter of any particular theological position. I recall classmates rehearsing their lines for ordination committees and boards while in seminary. It was shameless. Some folks would say whatever was necessary to get what they wanted just like a man with an erection. Both parties would be aware of what it was, but played along as they each had an agenda to advance.

The committee chair slammed her palms on the table and stood to reprimand me. "How dare you come in here and disagree with the discipline of our church?"

I clapped back with defiance, "How dare you invite me knowing in advance where I stand?"

She gave me that knowing look that I could lie my way into the next phase of the process like so many others have done before me. However, I fear God and would have to live with myself knowing I had. Integrity is clearly not one of their preferred character traits.

That was the end of the road for me. At least I could say I tried. If God wanted me to be ordained by human hands, it would have happened by now. I have made peace with the fact that it has not. Before I reached that point, however, I offered a shortlist of pastor friends a substantial amount of money to ordain me. They all jumped at the opportunity to get paid under the table for something they were not willing to do otherwise. Not only that, they began to outbid each other downward. That is when I had to question myself about the value of public perception.

The final lesson for me was that victory is not always visible. Over the years, I realized that I was more successful than many ministers with outward trappings of the profession. My character and faith are intact; people trust me; and I can look at myself comfortably in the mirror. In the meantime, my career resumed, my finances were restored, and life went on.

Attaining a license from the state or certificate from a denomination would no more qualify me than God has already. Of course, I had to go back to God to ask why I had to go through all I did. The answer resided in an old hymn of the church:

> When through fiery trials thy pathway shall lie,
>
> My grace, all-sufficient, shall be thy supply;
>
> The flame shall not harm thee; I only design
>
> Thy dross to consume and thy gold to refine.[29]

Knowing God was watching the entire scenario as it unfolded was the one thing that kept me grounded. I often wondered whether any of the other players were likewise mindful of God's omniscience. God not only knows, but holds us accountable for our actions.

Would receiving approval from a group of mere mortals validate my call even more? Do multiple rejections make me any less anointed? *[F]or God's gifts and [God's] call are irrevocable.* Who in the Bible had to get a second opinion after being called directly by The Almighty? In 1 Samuel 16, the Lord sent Samuel to Jesse the Bethlehemite to anoint one of his sons as the new King of Israel. *When they arrived, Samuel saw Eliab and thought, "Surely the Lord's anointed stands here before the Lord."* Although called and inspired by God, Samuel got it wrong. He eventually anointed Jesse's youngest son David as king. Kierkegaard described ordination as an "ostensible token, though not an infallible one."[30] Took me a long time to realize I have nothing to prove to anyone.

The Apostle Paul said: *But when God, who set me apart from my mother's womb and called me by his grace, was pleased to reveal his Son in me so that I might preach him among the Gentiles, my immediate response was not to consult any human being.* Why was I torturing myself?

Jesus came to usher in an unmediated faith, whereas the church tries to assume the role as gatekeeper to God. No experience grounded in God becomes terminal because of human intervention. It just gets delayed. As long as I have breath, I must keep pressing. My ministry did not begin with my entry into an ordination process. Neither did it end when the church denied me a position.

I also had to ask myself why I felt the need to formalize the context of my preaching. Prophets of old simply conveyed to the people what they heard from the Lord without any external validation. John the

Baptist preached what had been revealed to him and people gathered wherever he spoke. Jesus simply proclaimed truths as the Word that became flesh. All of these prophets were killed. None of these great men of God preached as much as the average pastor today. If one's preaching is not threatening the world's order true to the gospel, then it must be questioned.

Ordination and professional ministry are predictable routes. Embracing one's calling requires savoring mystery as a quintessential characteristic of God. Like almost everything else in life of which I was absolutely certain, the path to ordained ministry proved to be wrong for me. God called me to preach the gospel. That much I know. God did not call me to the systems of the world, even as they are manifest in the church. Yet, I kept trying in vain for their acceptance like Sisyphus.

There is a concept in economics called the Law of Diminishing Returns. In essence, it says for each additional unit of one input, there is a corresponding increase in another output until a certain point is reached. Hypothetically speaking, let's say for each hour you spend in church, you grow one unit spiritually. After a certain number of hours, say 10,000, growth plateaus and you are made no better or worse by attending church. After 15,000 hours, you actually begin to decline spiritually by one unit with each additional hour. After 20,000 hours, you become hell-bound. I use this illustration for effect, but it demonstrates the pattern of what happens to some people. That is why I do not hang out with preachers.

I actually sympathize with those in pastoral ministry. They approach the pulpit over 50 times a year with people expecting them to say something fresh, powerful, and life-changing from above. There is only so much material to work with. Even the best comedians have limited bits and travel the world sharing the same show with different audiences. A professor once said it would do his heart good to have a preacher approach the pulpit, tell those assembled "I got nothing," and cut the service short. I know it would do my heart good not to hear them struggle to fake it and step out of the limelight for a minute. It would also do the hearts good of those among them who are sitting on prophetic words.

So what if the institution does not accept one's call to ministry? The show must go on. Preach anyhow. If the process does not affirm what God has ratified already, then it is a lie. In the same vein, the process also approves those who do not proclaim to have a call from God. The pastor of my last congregation greeted a former member who was home visiting for the holidays from the pulpit. "We have been trying to call this young man to the ministry for years, but he won't go." Ironically, this pastor was known for blocking candidates for ordination more often than advancing them. I stepped to him after service. "You do know YOU cannot call ANYONE to ministry, right?" He looked at me like a deer caught in headlights. Then I had my answer.

I will never minimize the trauma anyone has experienced within a community of faith, for obviously I have been there myself. However, God is bigger than what anyone says about God or does in God's name. The power at work in believers makes it possible to transcend the weapons seeking to destroy our faith or inhibit the practice thereof. If the community of which you belong is not productive for you, then leave or even consider forming another.

There are times in one's life when one must depart from any relationship that proves to be detrimental. Anything less would be casting thy pearls before swine. I now know the source of my deliverance. It is not an organization. It is God. I know who called me. It was not the ecclesiastical leadership. It was God. I know who holds my future. It is not a denomination. It is God. My travails saved me from venerating men and women in high places to reserve my reverence for God alone. People will fail us. We will even fail ourselves at times. The truth of the matter is that even in the midst of those failures, God is still working things out for good.

11

ENDING THE MADNESS

Never let anything so fill you with sorrow as to make you forget the joy of the Christ risen.

Mother Teresa

On Good Friday of 2013, I took to the pulpit of Asbury United Methodist Church to preach one of the seven last words. Reflecting on Jesus' statements from the cross is a tradition dating back to the 16th Century. The service typically has a dramatic voiceover of quotes from our savior from the Passion accounts, along with seven brief homilies interspersed with thematic songs. Black churches are more predisposed to having an unabridged service because our experience is filled with so much suffering and we do not mind staying in church all day long. The climax is the fried fish dinner served afterward just as our Lord and Savior would have it.

Knowing how I felt about the denomination and it about me, I selected the sixth word as my swan song. *It is finished.* Goodbye. Sayonara. Hasta la vista, baby. As I prayed and studied in preparation, God revealed that verse was not my word to deliver. I called the pastor to request Jesus' fourth word from the cross as the Spirit led me. *My God, my God, why hast thou forsaken me?* He graciously assented.

Service had begun already when I begrudgingly entered the sanctuary. Despite my laborious preparation, part of me was dismissive of the congregation and wanted to skip it. The liturgical formalities were underway as the first preacher prepared to expound upon the first word. I slipped in from the side door below the pulpit and took a seat on the front pew wearing dark sunglasses, a black bodysuit, black wide-leg wool crepe pants, a long black leather coat, and black high-heeled boots because I was escaping from The Matrix.

The first sermon based on *Father, forgive them, for they do not know what they do* amounted to "Jesus is nice." Then came "We are all going to heaven" based on *Truly, I say to you, today you will be with me in paradise.* "We are all one big family" based on Jesus telling the Apostle John *Woman, behold your son. Son, behold your mother* came next. Each of the three messages had a sterile detachment from the emotions of the day as if the speakers' lives did not intersect with their sermons. My stomach tightened as I prepared to get all kinds of messy.

The fourth word was true to my feelings as I felt more abandoned by God in my attempts to pursue ministry as a profession than compelled to cheekily bid farewell to the church. My perspective on this familiar text was grounded in the writings of St. John of the Cross. The message had to be very personal to accurately reflect how the text resonated with my state at the time. I went deep into Scripture and deep into myself.

The sermon opened with a somber acknowledgement that Jesus was wise enough not to expect much from people in the first place. *But Jesus, on His part, was not entrusting Himself to them, for He knew all men, and because He did not need anyone to testify concerning man, for He Himself knew what was in man.* Humans are fallible and will let us down given enough opportunities. The disciples and the supporting cast of characters in the biblical narrative were just along for the ride. But Jesus expected more from the One who is not a man that He should lie. *My God, my God, why hast thou forsaken me?*

This was one of a few moments when the humanity of Jesus manifest powerfully. It was at this time that the paradox of his perfect union with God and necessity of taking on the sin of the world merged fully. This is what St. John of the Cross would call "the dark night of the soul." Occasions such as this are necessary in the life of the believer. St. John of the Cross said:

> No matter how much individuals do through their own efforts, they cannot actively purify themselves enough to be disposed in the least degree for the divine union of the perfection of love. God must take over and purge them in that fire that is too dark for them.[31]

At times when God is most intimately involved, it can seem like God is furthest removed. To be true to the verse and the moment, it was time for me to be transparent with my past hurt, present vulnerability, and ultimate sense of betrayal.

God called me to preach the gospel. I did not ask for this or assume the role of my own volition. Throughout my sermon preparation, and for that matter the previous seventeen years, I kept thinking about how my life would have been better in a lot of ways had God just left me alone. The institutional church blocked access to the profession consistently during my pursuit of ministry. I expected such from The Adversary. The world did not even have to torment me. But people calling themselves the Body of Christ have gone to extraordinary lengths to deny this one her rightful place in the kingdom.

Yes, bodies parading as the body get in God's way all the time. I recounted my experience with sexual harassment in the church during that sermon and how the initial shock threw me for the greatest existential loop I have ever experienced. I cried for years *My God, my God, why hast thou forsaken me?* In my agony, I still quit my job, moved to an unfamiliar city, struggled financially, remained loyal to the organized church, and studied like my life depended on it. To God's credit, I have always had provision, functioned as a member of society, and kept the faith.

My dark night taught me that God never leaves us. God only retreats to strengthen us for walking in divine power. I got over it seasonally, but my self-imposed quest for acceptance reopened the wounds. The Chair of the District Committee on Ordained Ministry looked me in the eye just a few weeks prior and told me I had "no place in ordained ministry in the United Methodist Church now or ever." She left no room for ambiguity. She tried to temper the harshness of her remarks by welcoming me to remain in fellowship. What she really meant was I was welcome to be pimped another way by continuing to give the church my money and free labor with nothing in return.

I had to decide whether I was going to clip my wings and reduce my presence to being a perpetual lay member or launch into a new beginning apart from the denomination. The former was not an option as Scripture commands us not to quench the spirit. Previous efforts to put the call behind me failed. It met me every morning I arose, followed me throughout the day, and gave me unrest at night. I was far less attached to this church after experiencing a long series of disappointments at others. Therefore, leaving was not too difficult.

Little did she know, I no longer cared about institutional approval. I addressed the Chair emphatically. "I do not support anything that does not support me!" She and the others around the table looked stunned that this little Black woman would come in there and sass them in such a manner. With that exchange, my fate with the United Methodist Church was consequently sealed.

I left the pulpit that day feeling ten feet tall not because I had taken the liberty to one up the church with my rhetorical lashing, but more so due to God advancing my ministry beyond the constraints of the institution. What was supposed to take me down turned out to be life-giving. As much as I am an avid church-goer, I strive to walk how Jesus did. When the two diverged, I had to choose. I chose the liberation Christ offers. Free spirits have to leave or become exhausted from continuous struggles to mold them.

People greeted me in a variety of ways at the conclusion of the service. The pastor made a beeline to me. "I know everybody on the Committee and not one of them could have preached that sermon."

I rolled my eyes and said, "well the church has made its preferences clear and deserves what it has."

The Bishop in Residence approached me next. "Your oratory was great, but I took exception with the personal parts."

I replied, "God did not direct me to you for advice or counsel during my preparation so you need to direct your objections to heaven." By no coincidence, he has been disciplined by the church in the past for sexual misconduct.

A guest musician blessed my soul by affirming the level of toil and inspiration he observed in my sermon. He followed me out of the sanctuary and said "your sermon was the only real word I heard today." That was not to say the other preachers did not prepare adequately. Rather, it was a commentary on how some preachers go through the motions without revealing their lived experience with Scripture. I have been guilty of such myself, but had the luxury of a present crisis and time to focus on it keenly. Another attendee emailed me to say the message was "exquisite, eloquent, and moving." The compliment blew me away as the mire of my experience actually produced something beautiful unbeknownst to me.

Members of the congregation were kind of skittish as I entered the fellowship hall where fish dinners were being served. Some shared the bishop's sentiments and preferred that I had not used the pulpit to air church business. That led me to change my mind about consuming food prepared by people who might harbor ill will against me. The most touching response came from my junior high school band director who was another guest musician for the service. He lamented learning I had such an experience and expressed admiration of my perseverance. A former girlfriend of his suffered from similar sexual harassment at the hands of a minister in charge of a faith-based recovery program. She relapsed as a direct result of the abuse and eventually died in a drug-related automobile collision.

There are many more out there suffering at the hands of those who should be fostering their spiritual journeys. For each person who walks away with their soul relatively intact, there are dozens of casualties. I have been held up as a poster child for what happens to those who are not complicit with their oppression. Ironically, I have never heard of a woman who had a problem getting ordained AFTER giving up the panties.

That is why my silence is not for sale. Whenever called to give an account for why I have not been ordained by the institution, I tell the truth. It is not because of any shortcoming of my own; it is because I do not play the game the way Christendom insists it be played. Of course, every denomination has a prohibition against such conduct. However, perpetrators seldom face any consequences.

During seminary, my church administration instructor, who was also the school's Bishop in Residence, recounted one of his experiences in ministry to our class. A white pastor under his charge in western North Carolina had an adulterous affair with a parishioner's wife. The bishop consequently assigned him to another congregation within the same Conference. The pastor committed the same offense at the next church. The bishop expressed dismay at the fact the husband at the second church sued him and the United Methodist Church successfully. I said reflexively, "He should have. You created the conditions for his victimization." The class gasped collectively like they sucked all the air out the room at my confronting this elderly white man in such an esteemed position—in the deep South, no less. The Bishop closed his leather portfolio abruptly, announced the dismissal of class, and stormed out the door. He offered to ordain me out of a sense of contrition when he learned of my plight.

A member of Asbury who happened to be a retired police officer told me not to think I can go around talking about sexual harassment and expect to receive the spoils of the institution. Her words were not intended to direct me one way or the other. Rather, she was simply acknowledging the cost of violating the purple code of silence.

Officers of the law have their unwritten blue code of silence which forbids them from speaking openly about the misconduct of their peers no matter how egregious. Other professions and closed societies have the same ethos embedded in their culture. Ask any corporate whistleblower how hard it was ever to find work again. Snitch and you suffer the consequences. Organized crime and organized religion are no different in culture. Violate omerta and you are dead to them. Such is nowhere to be found in Scripture. Only evil requires a veil of secrecy for its operations.

One day I got all excited to receive an email from a woman with whom I worked closely for several years at Asbury. A couple of years had passed since my departure. I sent her a personalized card following the passing of her husband and she responded with a written expression of gratitude. My joy deflated upon realizing her account had been hacked and the message was spam.

The perpetrator of my oppression and those who tacitly enabled his behavior have gone to great lengths to silence and discredit those like me lest such accounts force them to act. Ironically, neither sexual predators nor those who quietly relent face such dire penalties. If this is how the church gets down, then we are definitely not safe in the world.

I have been in church all my life and have not heard a single message against unscrupulous ministers from a pulpit—not one. That includes innumerable Sunday services, denominational conferences, ordination rites, pastoral installations, and yes, even seminary. We know lots about the Good Shepherd and *The Lord is my Shepherd*. However, we would be hard-pressed to find cautionary examples of who not to follow. Some Scripture is bad for business. What is a bad shepherd? Thus says the Lord:

> *Woe to the shepherds of Israel who only take care of themselves! Should not shepherds take care of the flock? You eat the curds, clothe yourselves with the wool and slaughter the choice animals, but you do not take care of the flock.*

If a pastor is fleecing his or her flock or demonstrating other untoward signs, there should be no expectation that they have the character to perform the loving works that good shepherding requires. I don't care how many turkeys they donate at Thanksgiving; their standard of living should not be far beyond the average member of the congregation if doing so comes at the mission's expense. Any believer witnessing ministerial malfeasance has an obligation to The One who knows all and sees all to address it, regardless of the consequences.

I have never been one to pursue ill-gotten gain. Therefore, the institutional church can keep its titles, frocks, and rewards. Well, maybe not the frocks. Most of what I miss is not that deep. Oswald Chambers offers a reminder. "To be shallow is not a sign of being wicked, nor is shallowness a sign that there are no deeps; the ocean has a shore."[32] It does not matter by what title I am called. I have managed to earn a living beyond the walls of the church. As a matter of fact, I never trusted them with my livelihood in the first place. But the fashionable things I could have done with a clerical collar remain to be seen.

I wish I could say I was holding out for something nobler than the opportunity to rock preacher swag. I am not into whooping and flashy cars, but I am quite a clothes horse. As I prepared for my initial sermon, what I would wear received more attention than what I would say. Each Sunday spent in the pulpit as a licentiate was a deliberate display of my eye for design. More than anything I studied more seasoned preachers to inform choices about my eventual clerical vestments and accessories.

Clerical vestments have their biblical origins in priestly attire. God provided very specific instructions in Levitical law for what the priests should wear down to their undergarments. In the same manner, I have both outer garments and intimate apparel that I consider divinely-inspired. One sister in ministry in the AME Church was a former buyer for high-end clothing at New York City retailers such as Bergdorf's and Saks. Albertine's fashion sense extended seamlessly to the garb of her second career. When she left the AME Church for the Episcopal Church, the seeming constraints of Anglicanism could not contain her invincible will to be stylish. She could rock a clerical collar with haute couture like no other. Excessive editing made the most exquisite pieces look like nothing. Ironically, so many others work hard to make far lesser attire appear to be much more.

Who knows what I would have become had I succeeded in being approved for clerical status by the institutional church? That would have left me to chart my own course for shaping my ministry according to the prevailing ethos. However, their cultural norms do not suit me. No denomination can function effectively with only unquestioning, complicit, and conforming members. Carl Jung said:

> A million zeroes joined together do not, unfortunately, add up to one. Ultimately everything depends on the quality of the individual, but our fatally shortsighted age thinks only in terms of large numbers and mass organizations, though one would think that the world had seen more than enough of what a well-disciplined mob can do in the hands of a single madman.[33]

This is a case in point where strength is not derived in large numbers. He goes further:

> People go on blithely organizing and believing in the sovereign remedy of mass action, without the least consciousness of the fact that the most powerful organizations in the world can be maintained only by the greatest ruthlessness of their leaders and the cheapest of slogans.[34]

That is totally not me. I have never been a follower.

My treatment by the church is reminiscent of a scene in the movie *One Flew Over the Cuckoo's Nest*. A longtime resident of a psychiatric hospital tells the protagonist, Randle McMurphy, (played by Jack Nicholson), "they work on you harder because you are strong." McMurphy was actually faking insanity to avoid prison. The leadership agreed to keep him institutionalized not because they identified a particular psychiatric diagnosis requiring treatment. Rather, they were accepting the challenge of subduing him, thus being self-perpetuating. In the end, McMurphy succumbed to excessive treatment within the institution and actually became insane.

This demonstrates the effects of institutionalization. Being self-perpetuating plays out in real life as well. Psychologist David Rosenhan performed an experiment whereby eight sane people were admitted secretly to twelve different hospitals in five states across the United States. The subjects all confessed to hearing voices and expressed existential angst. The pseudopatients stopped reporting signs of mental illness immediately upon admission, but had to convince the staff to declare them sane for release. "Length of hospitalization ranged from 7 to 52 days, with an average of 19 days. The pseudopatients were not, in fact, carefully observed, but this failure clearly speaks more to traditions within psychiatric hospitals than to lack of opportunity."[35] Getting released proved more challenging than expected. And so it is with the church.

Once again, God saved me from myself. I was totally down with joining the dog and pony show not knowing the cost. Very early in my experience, the church's ethics revealed themselves not to be higher than secular ones. They talked a good game, but the truth of the matter was on full display. No one was going to forcibly expel me or tell me to leave as long as my presence suited their interests. The choice became very clear. Either I had to sweep my story under the rug and perpetuate the hypocrisy or forcefully reject a pattern of behavior that has to be as offensive to God as it is to me.

Church, bye!

12

RELEASING THE RESTRAINTS

Where there is a lull of truth, an institution springs up. But the truth blows right on over it, nevertheless, and at length blows it down.

Henry David Thoreau

Remaining in the faith requires a degree of insanity for basing the pattern of one's entire life on a man rising from the grave over 2,000 years ago. There's no way around that. However, God does not want believers to abandon all reason. Jesus warned his disciples. *I am sending you out like sheep among wolves. Therefore be as shrewd as serpents and as innocent as doves.* Resurrection faith opens a whole new realm of thought that makes the impossible possible. Only the foolishness of the cross empowers the mind. Man-made foolery—the likes of which never ceases to amaze—insults the intelligence and ultimately leads to destruction.

People have inquired about the source of my resilience. Many times, have I been asked whether I considered quitting. Invariably, I acknowledge that I have more times than they can imagine. Of course, the Holy Spirit gets most of the credit for my staying power. She believed for me when I exceeded my natural capacity for faith. Another source is my name. There is a lot to a name. (Be careful what you name your children). So many times, I wondered myself why I did not crumble and die in the midst of my trials.

Then one Saturday afternoon I found the answer while spending the day at the Metropolitan Museum of Art. (Do I know how to party or what?) Taking the train to New York City for the weekend became a form of escapism whenever therapy became too intense. I would treat myself to shopping, fine dining, museum hopping, and the theater as a diversion. Never did I announce my visits to my many friends who lived there. As a matter of fact, they had no idea what I was going through.

My name—Dionne—is derived from Dionysus, the Greek god of wine, revelry, theater, and religious ecstasy. Yes, I am well acquainted with drinking, partying, performing (I am an alum of the Washington Improv Theater and appeared in a local production of The Vagina Monologues), and have had encounters with the divine. However, the most compelling aspect of our relationship is embedded in the myth surrounding his life.

Dionysus translates as "that which cannot be destroyed." Legend holds that attempts were made to kill him from the time Hera discovered a mortal maiden, Semele, was carrying her husband Zeus' love child. She tormented Dionysus continuously and enlisted Zeus' brother Hades to destroy him. This ongoing enmity continued with the god of the underworld throughout Dionysus' lifetime.

I pined for death like anyone prone to depression experiencing an existential crisis. My thoughts wandered from why random tragedy had not yet killed me to serious consideration of ending it all myself. Being a believer in providence, my time had not yet come. No meteors have fallen from the sky crushing me. No trucks wiped me out during my frequent jaywalking. That is not to mention my unexplained protection while being the road warrior I am. Although I have had scares with endometrial and breast cancer over the years, both biopsies returned benign results. Two consecutive years have not passed since affirming my calling without some major disappointment, setback, or misfortune. Every time I feel like I'm riding high, trouble looms around the next corner.

Being a great procrastinator, my mood and will never coincided. I dare not divulge my specific ideations of suicide. The last time, I was riding my bicycle and chose a date. As I rounded the next curve, a wind wiped me out as if God slapped the thought out of my mind. I hit the ground so hard, my head bounced slowly on the pavement three times.

Fortunately, I was wearing a helmet as my mother always warned me to do.

As I laid on the bike path disoriented, I thought not to get up—ever. Had the pavement swallowed me at the moment, I would have been fine with it. A fellow rider extended a hand and lifted me from the ground after I did not respond. A crowd began to gather and I wept despite my attempt at stoic restraint. Raised never to make a scene in public, I got back on my bike and followed the path to my car at a measured pace. I sat in the driver's seat in silence knowing despair was not the place for me despite life sucking miserably at that time with no reversal in sight.

The more I reflected on the life of my mythical namesake, the more I knew my story would not end in defeat. Romans 8:28 tells us *God causes all things to work together for good to those who love God, to those who are called according to [God's] purpose.* The call of God is the one thing I cannot deny. Trust me, I have tried. Just as Hades and Dionysus were mired in a struggle, I have been going through hell trying to fulfill God's will for my life. Enduring the trials until I hit my high note has been the hardest part. But as Winston Churchill said: If you're going through hell, keep going.

My final departure from institutional religion came after twelve years at the church I joined after seminary. God led me to Asbury, so I went and felt at home. It was good while it lasted despite conflicts with The Replacement pastor and the effect of accounts of sexual harassment in my previous denomination. After a third thwarted attempt at ordination, I struck out with professional ministry and organized religion as a whole.

Ironically, it would have been much less challenging for me to pursue more shady vocations in the world than ordained ministry. I could have easily been a hooker, drug dealer, stripper, used car salesperson, multilevel marketing mogul, pharmaceutical sales representative, or heaven forbid a politician. The church does the kingdom a disservice by straining so many gnats with its superfluous criteria, while swallowing camels that give the church a bad name. The old me would have given up the panties for less. There is no doubt I have been changed.

The most powerful revelation came when God told me I did not belong to those systems anyway.

And no one puts new wine into old wineskins; otherwise the new wine will burst the skins and it will be spilled out, and the skins will be ruined. But new wine must be put into fresh wineskins. And no one, after drinking old wine wishes for new; for he says, "The old is good enough."

This passage always confounded me up until that point because I had not become transformed fully. It was not until I was sufficiently regenerated and allowed the Holy Spirit to lead me in all matters did the scales fall from my eyes. Notice the transformation has taken place with the subject in the passage—new wine, i.e., the born-again believer. It is the context and structure in which the transformed substance is placed—the institution—that remains unchanged. Jesus never tried to change the religious establishment of his day. Neither were they receptive to God incarnate. He created anew in me just as the prophets of old promised. Hence, there was no way I could remain where God did not intend and claim to be in right relationship with the divine.

The most valuable book for me as I recovered from my drama with the church was *People of the Lie.* It is a disturbing account of the psychology of faith-based communities, describing how evil permeates the religious realm as it becomes increasingly organized. Of course, no one in the church recommended the book. You will not hear of any group studies on it. If you have ever been through anything in the church you, will recognize the wreckage and find its analysis therapeutic.

The author, M. Scott Peck, postulates that we do things as part of a whole that we would never do individually. There is something compromising about being part of a group or wanting to do so. Anyone who pledged a fraternity or sorority (old school) can attest to the insanity of desiring to belong. On the front-end, they draw the line on how far they would go in pursuit of popularity, enhanced status, and networking opportunities. Once a person is in the mix and the prize is within view, there is little they will not do. Some have experienced emotional and psychological abuse, alcohol poisoning, physical injury, and even death in pursuit of membership in Greek-lettered organizations that espouse principles contrary to all of these activities.

Evil loves institutions. "So as they become larger and larger, our institutions become absolutely faceless and soulless. What happens when there is no soul? Is there just a vacuum? Or is there Satan where once a soul resided?"[36] When people get locked inside institutions, they lose sight of their own values and adopt those of what they consider larger than themselves. The illusion of nobility supersedes moral integrity. That's where cognitive dissonance intervenes.

Going to church for many is like a gentleman's agreement to live a lie. I had a lover in my young adult years with whom I never discussed sex although we had plenty of it. We made plans to meet for an array of activities, always knowing how it would end. He would say "Let's go to the movies." "Want to come over to watch the game?" "I have a new flavor of ice cream." I would be right there with little interest in the overt offer. I knew what it was, but played along for my own indulgence.

Along the same lines, it pained me to no end to see people I loved and respected as passive bystanders knowing the character of the perpetrator. "That's just the way it is" was the common refrain. For that reason, more than a few women have slept for their papers because no one was going to help them get them any other way. So much for the Good Samaritan. Help a victim, forget high-profile preaching engagements, sought-after appointments, and other perks of the institution. Worship has become a spectator sport with less interest in being armed to fight the Lord's battles than superficial affiliation with the kingdom of God.

"Deindividuation is characterized as a state of lowered (private) self-awareness and self-regulation in a group. The result of this state is antinormative behavior: acts that violate established norms of appropriateness."[37] In other words, we lose ourselves after we become engrained in a larger social framework. Church members and people functioning within institutions become deindividuated by immersion into their group affiliation. As such, they adopt values in conflict with their own. Members actively and passively tolerate malfeasance in organizations or groups with which they identify that they would reject on an individual basis. However, group norms override their personal objections when they occur in a broader context. When those group norms become harmful, counterproductive, or objectionable one must assess whether the organization is a good fit for them.

Well, like Paul, *I do not regard myself as having taken hold of it yet; but one thing I do: forgetting what lies behind and reaching forward to what lies ahead, I press on toward the goal for the prize of the upward call of God in Christ Jesus.* Twenty-five years after first entering the ordination process, I still have no papers but my integrity is intact. My preaching engagements are few and far between and I do not get invited to do much else. However, I sleep well at night. *For what shall it profit a [woman], if [she] shall gain the whole world, and lose [her] own soul?* There will be no shortage of preachers and self-satisfied religious types in hell and they will have a lot of familiar company.

I attended the funeral of one of my beloved sisters in Christ at Asbury soon after leaving. Frequent queries about when I planned to return drained the life out of me. I left for a reason. They all know what it is. That reason has not been resolved. I felt like shaking each person by their shoulders as they claimed to love and miss me out of one side of their mouth, while refusing to put themselves on the line to resolve my exclusion from full-fledged ministry out the other. Why would they think I would reduce myself to a spiritual bonsai tree to be in the club? That is exactly what membership there would amount to without manifesting the life to which I have been called.

Yes, I do enjoy their company and find the worship services entertaining. But how can I participate fully without exercising my gifts? More than that, why would they find it a reasonable proposition? In the Parable of the Sower, Jesus tells of a laborer being chastised for not using his talents. Elsewhere, Scripture says *do not quench the Spirit.* Rejoining that congregation would require a certain degree of psychosis to detach from the calling that is intrinsically part of me and what they claim to know about what God requires. Honestly, my absence bothers them less than having exiles in the street.

People confide in me quite frequently that they do not get involved deeply in their communities of faith because they do not want to know about the evil that lurks therein. That is no different than turning a blind eye, thus aiding and abetting said evil. It is incumbent on every believer to confront evil if you know, or even suspect, it exists around you. If you cannot do that, then you must leave lest you too have blood on your hands.

The good news is that not all churches or organizations are evil. However, they present the conditions for evil to flourish the more they become institutionalized. We make choices as a part of a collective that we would never make singularly, especially when there is a reward involved. It can be money, a promotion, elevated social status, or something as simple as recognition. The tendency toward evil becomes greater as the reward and level of anonymity increase with the size and strength of the organization.

The most shameful thing is that people have created gods they consider higher than the crown of Christ. *They exchanged the truth of God for a lie, and worshiped and served created things rather than the Creator— who is forever praised.* The rub is not that we all sellout on some level on a regular basis, but most of us have not yet been offered a high enough price for our souls. I must admit I wanted to win more than I wanted the actual prize. Shedding the perception of losing was more important than a certificate or particular position. The more I interact with my friends serving in institutional church roles, the more I am grateful not to be in their shoes. Many have actually expressed a longing to change places with me because of my freedom, disposable income, and leisure time. One's existential position before God is far more important than anything an institution can bestow.

Thomas Moore's advice is on point. "You have to be faithful to the mystery taking place in your heart, rather than to any idea or system that would try, with the best of motives, to disempower you and make you theirs."[38] The institution did not accept me without my conforming to what it needed me to be. "To thine own self be true" as Shakespeare wrote in Hamlet. In today's parlance, that translates to keeping it real. Philosopher Martin Heidegger describes human beings as being capable of only one sin: inauthenticity. Each of us was created with a divine purpose. Not fulfilling it places us in a state of rebellion against God.

Fortunately, my hope is not built on any individual, organization, or earthly thing. If it were, it would fail every time. However, I am crazy enough to believe there is so much more to God than any single person, object, or concept can capture. When those things fail, God meets me. Faith is a huge risk because there is always a chance one is wrong. But nothing ventured, nothing gained. Its reward is not all material; it is a higher state of being that defies explanation. We must allow a little madness into our lives, but take it with a grain of salt.

I found comfort in my studies to learn I am not the first person in the history of the world to feel this way. Scripture is replete with examples of how universal the struggle of keeping the faith is. *No temptation has overtaken you except what is common to mankind. And God is faithful; he will not let you be tempted beyond what you can bear. But when you are tempted, he will also provide a way out so that you can endure it.* The psalmists also pondered the futility of faithfulness while the wicked prospered.

> *Do not fret because of evildoers,*
> *Be not envious toward wrongdoers.*
> *For they will wither quickly like the grass*
> *And fade like the green herb.*
> *Trust in the Lord and do good;*
> *Dwell in the land and cultivate faithfulness.*
> *Delight yourself in the Lord;*
> *And He will give you the desires of your heart.*

Only a few generations into the early church, young believers separated themselves from the emerging institution for the simple life of monasticism. Theologians have shone light on ecclesiastical fallacies throughout the ensuing centuries. Africans in the bondage of enslavement separated the wheat from the chaff to find liberation in the religion imposed to control them. Radical activists formed a praxis to advance social change. And now I must be the gospel so God can do a new thing to set Godself free from that which never held the divine in the first place. I am in the pulpit wherever I go. Nobody can stop me from preaching.

13

EMANCIPATION

But I think my dream would be to find a group of people who would sign on the dotted line that they intend never to become an institution.

Barbara Brown Taylor

One of the greatest miracles in my life is that I still believe. I did not even recognize this until one day I said so while catching up with one of my seminary professors about a decade after graduation. No, studying theology did not cause me to lose faith. Rather, it helped me to maintain it while everything around me seemed not to conform with what I had been taught about God and life in Christ. All of my previous leanings had to die so a new, reimagined faith could emerge.

The single thing that was abundantly clear was God did not call me to a building, an ideology, or a group of people. Surprisingly, God did not call me to wear a couture robe or divinely-inspired jewelry either. God called me into relationship with the divine. Tattered jeans and comfort sandals have become my preferred uniform, along with wild, unprocessed tresses. My new look resembles a certain Galilean more than the formal vestments I once coveted. This renewed relationship has brought me into community with other people with similar experiences, but by no means confines me to an institution.

That begs the question of what the church is anyway. The Greek word *ekklesia*, translated as church, means "to gather." The church is therefore the collective people who have experienced the transcendent power of the risen Christ. *Now the Lord is that Spirit: and where the Spirit of the Lord is, there is liberty.* The church's gathering nature does not imply a static cohesion. Its power is in the going out to transform the world.

Communities claiming faith in Christ regressed into temple culture because it is easier to sell. Being born again produces a discursive shift in the orientation of one's life, resulting in a noticeable behavioral effect. The early church was the gathering of people after experiencing such a conversion. Believers initially greeted each other by inquiring "Have you been changed?"

Just as group membership can make us prone to evil, it can also ground us in the ideals of the organization. The latter makes us better than we otherwise would be by nurturing that which empowers us to live according to those ideals. In the modern era, organizational affiliation and family of origin have replaced transformation as symbolic of our standing before God. Most church members remain Christians in name only. Hence, so much hell is in the church.

It is no small wonder that church sanctuaries in America have expanded over the past few decades. We like everything big: big-box stores selling things we do not need; mega multiplex theaters showing very little worth seeing; sports arenas that can seat the entire population of a small town; and large-scale chain restaurants serving broad, unappetizing menus to our ever-widening derrieres. The church is gravitating in the same direction to accommodate the masses. It seems most churches have perpetual building campaigns. Doing so makes little sense from the perspective that these massive buildings will find themselves in the lake of fire when this world meets its end.

In early recorded history, people tried to reach God by building ziggurats. Genesis 11 provides the account of the Tower of Babel, which the builders thought could serve as a stairway to heaven. The first problem was the action was not commanded by God. The people did so to make a name for themselves among mortals not to improve their standing with their creator. They also mistook physical proximity to the sky for an indicator of their relationship with the divine. God consequently divided their languages to prevent collaboration on such futile efforts.

As God led the Hebrew children from bondage in Egypt to the Promised Land, God ordered the priests to maintain a tent of meeting as a portable dwelling place symbolizing God's presence among them. Jerusalem was a sacred place in Israel because it was thought God lived there. Psalm 46:4 calls Jerusalem *the City of God, The holy dwelling places of the Most High.* God later ordered the building of the Temple in Jerusalem as a sacred space for the Israelites' worship and ritualistic activities.

Solomon, the wisest man ever to live, was quick to acknowledge the limits of the building upon his completion of the temple. *But will God indeed dwell on the earth? Behold, heaven and the highest heaven cannot contain You, how much less this house which I have built!* Paul confirms this in the context of the New Testament. *The God who made the world and all things in it, since [God] is Lord of heaven and earth, does not dwell in temples made with hands.*

The temple served its purpose, but was by no means to be considered God's only presence in the world. Neither was it immune from God's wrath. The prophet Jeremiah warned that God would destroy the temple if the trust of the people became misplaced:

> *While you were doing all these things, declares the Lord, I spoke to you again and again, but you did not listen; I called you, but you did not answer. Therefore, what I did to Shiloh I will now do to the house that bears my Name, the temple you trust in, the place I gave to you and your ancestors. I will thrust you from my presence, just as I did all your fellow Israelites, the people of Ephraim.*

Although the temple was sacred and special, it was by no means absolute. From the very beginning, people violated its sanctity and misconstrued God's purpose for it. King Josiah's reforms included destroying *the houses of the male cult prostitutes which were in the house of the Lord* in Chapter 23 of 2 Kings. Not only that, when the temple was eventually destroyed and the Israelites were in exile and captivity, they fell into despondency as if the divine were no longer present.

Jesus came as the embodiment of a new temple. Mary and Joseph took baby Jesus to the temple to consecrate him to God, as required by the Law. Jesus made its importance abundantly clear from his childhood.

He lingered behind at the Temple in Jerusalem as Mary and Joseph made their way back home from celebrating the Passover. After journeying for a day, they doubled back to the city to find a snarky adolescent greeting them. *Why is it that you were looking for Me? Did you not know that I had to be in My Father's house?*

Jesus also revealed his identity early in his ministry at a synagogue in Galilee by reading from the Prophet Isaiah:

> *"The Spirit of the Lord is upon Me,*
>
> *Because He anointed Me*
>
> *to preach the gospel to the poor.*
>
> *He has sent Me to proclaim release to the captives,*
>
> *And recovery of sight to the blind,*
>
> *To set free those who are oppressed,*
>
> *To proclaim the favorable year of the Lord."*
>
> *And He closed the book, gave it back to the attendant and sat down; and the eyes of all in the synagogue were fixed on Him. And He began to say to them, "Today this Scripture has been fulfilled in your hearing."*

Jesus frequented the temple and used temple imagery in his language that flew over the heads of not only the religious leaders of his day, but also his own disciples. When asked to provide a sign proving his authority to perform miracles, *Jesus answered them, "Destroy this temple, and in three days I will raise it up.* He was even mocked from the cross with reminders of his claim. *And those passing by were speaking abusively to Him, shaking their heads, and saying, "You who are going to destroy the temple and rebuild it in three days, save Yourself! If You are the Son of God, come down from the cross."* While it is easy for us to stand on the other side of the resurrection and view them with disdain, we still do not comprehend that Jesus freed us from the confines of a temple.

Jesus issued The Great Commission, his final teaching, after his resurrection and before his Ascension. *Go therefore and [teach] all the nations, baptizing them in the name of the Father and the Son and the Holy Spirit, teaching them to observe all that I commanded you; and lo, I am with you always, even to the end of the age.* Jesus' finished work on the cross was the perfect sacrifice fulfilling the ritualistic requirements for atoning for sin. The new covenant unified what was scattered in response to earlier attempts to get to God in the temporal realm. The ushering in of the Spirit at Pentecost formed solidarity in believers unto this day to be God's presence in the world. This was the birth of the church not the construction of a building.

Ezekiel 37:26-27 establishes that a time will come when God will make a new covenant with humanity and dwell permanently with God's people. *I will make a covenant of peace with them; it will be an everlasting covenant with them. And I will place them and multiply them, and will set My sanctuary in their midst forever. My dwelling place also will be with them; and I will be their God, and they will be My people.*

The book of Revelation refers to "New Jerusalem" as the ideal state restored to God's order permanently. The second verse of the 21st Chapter describes the New Jerusalem as *the holy city, coming down out of heaven from God.* The writer further uses language to describe it as intimate fellowship that God has promised to those in covenant with the Holy One. New Testament scholar Robert Gundry takes a bold step in saying "John is not describing the eternal dwelling place of saints; he is describing them, and them alone."[39]

In other words, the New Jerusalem is not a heavenly city; it is the fleshly temples of those who believe. This newness raises saints to the cause of Christ beyond temporality and worldliness. Apostle Paul makes it very clear in I Corinthians 6:19. *Do you not know that your bodies are temples of the Holy Spirit, who is in you, whom you have received from God? You are not your own?*

Knowing all that we know, why are we building wider spatially rather than going deeper into ourselves? Christians have returned to primacy of the temple in the community of faith as opposed to being God's presence in the world. Some churches are housed on sprawling multi-acre campuses. Just as one mega church is complete, here come plans for others as some pastors get caught in the throes of steeple envy. Others view the relative success of large land-holding churches and follow suit with the belief "if we build it, they will come." Some churches are able to balance discipleship, witness, and charity on a large scale. However, they are fewer and farther between what we would like to believe.

Church membership has become a very transient affair. You can't swing a dead cat without hitting a big beautiful church in most metropolitan areas. Some are so immodest they command you to come inside and take a peek. A hard truth that congregations everywhere are learning is that people are drawn to new edifices in a sensory manner. A church can be the flavor of the month until the next bigger and more beautiful one is built. Then who is left holding the bag?

Just as owners of McMansions are finding themselves overextended, so are the McChurches. Religious institutional borrowing and building followed the same boom as residential and commercial development in the late 1990s through the first decade of the 2000s. Just as the subsequent effects of the economic downturn and financial risk have hit individuals, foreclosure proceedings against churches tripled in the second decade of the 2000s. Over 100 churches filed bankruptcy in 2010 alone. That is not to mention the effects of the COVID-19 pandemic.

Some jurisdictions have passed measures limiting the proportion of land used for religious organizations within them because their tax-exempt status does not improve the state's coffers. Some churches consider this a form of modern persecution, when in fact the government might be saving them from themselves. Few congregations or denominations are self-reflective enough to right-size their organizations. Perpetual growth seems to be the goal regardless of the needs of the community or financial sustainability. Just as the hubris of reaching God vertically led to a failed tower, the image of success has become the strongest selling point for some churches to capture their share of the market for believers.

The question remains about what type of body will arise. Jesus built no buildings, asked nobody for money, nor did he limit himself to one geographic location or social group. His ministry is beyond compare in terms of longevity, reach, and transformation of the world. How many modern ministries—Christian and otherwise—can say the same?

I cannot tell you the number of times a fellow preacher approached me excited about the innovative ministry they were conceptualizing only to have it become another version of the same ole same ole once it materialized. The gospel is not that complicated. Jesus came to redeem the fallen world. We who are saved are the first fruits of redemption. We will not know who will or will not receive ultimate salvation until He comes again.

Notice how biblical accounts always have people shocked when they arrive at either heaven or hell. St. Augustine also wrote centuries ago about the invisible, unpredictable church destined for heaven and the hell-bound religious masses. That removes the selling point of most churches who would like you to believe if you join them, not only will you have an aesthetically pleasing setting for your personal events, but also a guaranteed ticket to heaven.

The evidence of God's presence and activity in the world is embodied in those who are God's emissaries. We still bear the scars even after our recovery from trauma experienced in communities of faith. Rose Fitzgerald Kennedy is known for her thoughts on pain and healing. "It has been said that time heals all wounds. I don't agree. The wounds remain. Time—the mind, protecting its sanity—covers them with some scar tissue and the pain lessens, but it is never gone." Even after Jesus rose from the grave, he bore the marks of the thorns, nails, and whips. God could have easily erased them, but they remained to show forth the working of God's power. So it is with God's children.

We must not be so quick to dismiss the painful experiences of others at the hand of the church. We must likewise be discerning in our selection of communities of faith. Well-appointed edifices, entertaining music, and well-heeled members do not necessarily make for an edifying experience. They do, however, make lovely backdrops for weddings, funerals, name-dropping, and networking. My father is mad at me for leaving my historic downtown Washington congregation as he wanted to have his funeral there. We still can for a price. Temples were not originally intended to be venues for life's milestones. Weddings were held in community as unions between families and not necessarily religious observances. A corpse was also one of the most profane things to bring into consecrated space in Judaism. The construction of awe-inspiring sanctuaries changed that.

There is so much more to God and God's activity in the world than what is written in Scripture. Learning to think theologically was the first step to freeing my mind from the world of absolutes imposed upon me. Unyielding adherence to Torah became a stumbling block to the

Apostle Paul. According to Deuteronomy 21:22, *cursed is the one who hangs on a tree.* The very act of being crucified supposedly disqualified Jesus from being able to redeem the world. Anyone claiming Jesus as Messiah was to be persecuted for heresy. Paul did just that with zeal prior to his conversion.

An experience with the risen Christ liberated those who considered the law unimpeachable to be able to reconcile Torah with a new move of God. Paul's Damascus Road experience eradicated the offense of the cross, taking him from one of the fiercest enemies of the church to the most impactful proponent of the gospel. He wrote in Galatians 3:13 that *Christ redeemed us from the curse of the Law, having become a curse for us.* I likewise yielded to the Holy Spirit and cast off the black and white shackles in favor of a new vision of what God demands of me. The church tends to follow, rather than lead, revolutionary movements with its rigidity. *And do not be conformed to this world, but be transformed by the renewing of your mind, so that you may prove what the will of God is, that which is good and acceptable and perfect.* Recycled thinking, expressions, and operations impede the work of the Holy Spirit.

Most of the time it is not even Scripture or theology to which Christians are clinging. It is the collective traditions and political will of the organization. Christendom will fight even the Holy Spirit tooth and nail to preserve its own notions of faith. "Personal revelation [is] suspect because it bypassed dogma and the authority of the clergy. You can't have people voicing personal revelations that might bring down the whole house of cards."[40]

Abandoning communities of faith is not an option. I considered forming a virtual church on the Internet after my blog, "The Mad Theologian," gained momentum. However, there is no church without direct contact with people. *And the Word became flesh, and dwelt among us, and we saw His glory, glory as of the only begotten from the Father, full of grace and truth.*

Jesus could have phoned it in, so to speak, and effected redemption remotely from the heavens. Instead, he came to earth at a particular point in time, in a body, interacted with mortals, suffered, died, and rose again. While he was here, he also made a point to participate in organized religion. He did not need it and actually spoke vehemently against it. However, he demonstrated its importance to us by making appearances. Most importantly, he limited his exposure by being present far more in community than in the temple. And the Pharisees thought less of him for it too.

The bottom line is this: Jesus is coming back again for a church, not individuals. Believers are members of a body and each one is essential to its optimal functioning. That body is not confined to a building, organization, or ideology. There is more of God outside of any religious construct than within the invisible restraints used to bind believers. Finding the right balance is a personal pursuit for which religious activities are no proxy. Going to either extreme—apathy or fanaticism—is equally destructive. The church as we know it is vital for nurturing faith. However, it is not an end unto itself.

Without the church, there would have been no canonization and preservation of the Scriptures. Without the church, there would have been no collective witness to the power and effect of the resurrection. Without the church, there would not have been informed conversations about living by Christian faith. Without church, there would be no hymnals assembling common experiences throughout the generations set to music. Without church, I would not have been nurtured sufficiently to be able to write this book. Instead, I would likely be in a padded room somewhere wearing a straightjacket.

God never intended for faith to be a solitary endeavor. Yes, we all stand singularly in God's presence with fear and trembling. We must also stand individually before the throne in judgement on That Day. However, teaching, witness, and worship are interactive. I cannot imagine attaining faith without the strong tradition of saints who captured memories, established communities, and cultivated the atmosphere that would birth generations of disciples. From members of the early church who preserved documents that became Scripture to the patient ladies who taught me every week in Sunday School, a great cloud of witnesses saw to it that I grew in grace. Therefore, it is incumbent upon me to return the favor.

My expectations of life in Christian communities were exalted to say the least. I believed them to be the place where I was safe, loved, and free from the troubles of the world. If I have learned nothing else, the soul gets saved but the flesh does not. People ask me all the time whether I will join another congregation (usually with their own in mind). Until I find an environment supportive of my experience, healing, and continued growth, I will curtail my exposure. Otherwise, I would not be offering myself as the living sacrifice God commands, but merely presenting a shell of myself. The organized church welcomes me as long as it benefits their agenda, but ironically not God's will. Their primary agenda is to maintain the institution not to advance the kingdom.

Again, humanity puts the insanity in organized religion. I have discussed my examination of this subject with acquaintances whose faith traditions differ from mine. Their experiences have been strikingly similar. This point crystallized for me while taking a taxi home from the airport as I returned from a writers' workshop. The driver was from Eritrea, a small country in northeastern Africa. Upon hearing of my subject matter, he described dynamics in his community of faith back home that fits the mold of American Christendom well. I encouraged him to keep the faith in spite of it and he seemed convinced to do so.

I have had two dogs of my own. The first was a Pomeranian I purchased from a breeder. Knowing I planned to move from DC to Atlanta within a couple months, I left her there until my departure. The breeder took Trixie to her beach house on the Eastern Shore of Maryland every weekend until I assumed custody. Her life from that point forward was nothing short of charmed. Trixie was crate-trained and came to know its confines as her safe place. Once she was housebroken fully, I removed the door and she chilled in it at will. Whenever visiting another residence with a pet crate, Trixie was known to commit herself to it.

On the other hand, my Chihuahua is a rescue from a shelter. I do not know her full history, but became her third owner when she was only ten months-old. Phoebe treats any cage like Guantanamo Bay. She enters with great resistance and makes a break the first chance she gets. Clearly, she has been through some things. Her response to being confined is no reflection of her view of me, but rather a form of self-preservation. Phoebe is a survivor.

In the same manner, those for whom every day has been Sunday in the church welcome the opportunity to envelop themselves in its walls. Those who have felt a real or perceived threat at the hands of religious institutions are less likely to become a part of another. Fixed boundaries represent something different to each. Neither is right or wrong. People respond to stimuli based on their hardwiring and experience. We must respect the particularity of each person's spiritual journey and allow the Holy Spirit to redirect as God so wills.

So it should be with the church. The goal never should be simply to enlist people on the rolls as if they are objects for acquisition. Churches are God's household of faith. They should model the radical love ethic Jesus taught, not social institutions that take no accountability for the welfare of others. Jesus' adherents were passionate, unyielding, and even willing to follow him to death. Millie Jackson recorded a song called "Hot Wild Unrestricted Crazy Love." Its lyrics are not appropriate to quote here, but the essence of the title should be aspirational for the church.

There have been times when I shared some pretty intimate crises in Christian fellowship only to be faced with warmed over platitudes or cold indifference. Love is as love does. The church is supposed to demonstrate it differently than the world. But we are not to limit our practice of faith to the confines of the membership, edifice, or organization. Love unconditionally. Love extravagantly. Love without regard to otherness.

Jesus ordered believers to *go therefore into the world and [disciple] all nations,* not go to a building at regular intervals to serve one another. Coming together is important, but the world will be transformed by the sending forth of empowered believers demonstrating what love can do. Church should be a launching pad into a life of discipleship and service, not a terminal destination as members of an institution. Yes, feelings will get hurt. People will not live up to expectations. And terrible things will be done in God's name. Yet, there is still a divine power at work that is making all things new. What that means for me and my unbounded faith remains to be seen and I am finally at peace with not knowing.

> *The wind blows wherever it pleases. You hear its sound, but you cannot tell where it comes from or where it is going. So it is with everyone born of the Spirit.*

AFTERWORD

Writing this book was like being in labor for twenty years. My experience with organized religion weighed heavily on me and I earnestly hoped for a different outcome to my pursuit of a full spiritual experience. Very few churched people were shocked to hear my accounts. I have not described anything new here. This project has merely given expression to what has been trapped unutterably inside many souls.

I cannot explain why I still believe except to say my experience of God has been greater than those things done in God's name. As much as I would like to deny how downright lifeless and evil Christendom can be, it would amount to nothing but a lie. Both the world and its members know the church for what it is. I have spent more of my life than I am willing to admit being an apologist for that which is inexcusable.

I have been asked more times than a thousand whether I would have pursued ministry had I known at the time of the call what I know now. The human answer is "of course not." No sane person would risk financial stability, mental health, and personal relationships for the sake of what may not be true. That's why God concealed the path ahead of me like so many other things in life.

That brings me back to my original proposition. God made it abundantly clear to me that God is real and redemption is serious work. I cannot tell you the number of times I prayed for God to *remove this cup from me: nevertheless, not my will, but Thine, be done.* Abandoning the work to which God called me was not mine to do. So, I stayed the course, as I understood it, each step of the way.

I never counted the financial burden of attending seminary until my exit interview presented my accumulated debt head-on. Abandonment to Christ fixed my gaze otherworldly. As I walked on water, so to speak, I never took stock of the cost of my sacrifice. Coming face-to-face with what my discipleship cost me in dollars and cents was like a bucket of ice water in my face. That is not to mention the foregone income from leaving my professional life for three years. Although, I was no longer a part of the institution that required it, I was still on the hook for paying the bill. There was a lot of cussing and gnashing of teeth each month when I made those student loan payments. To the glory of God, I satisfied my debt well ahead of schedule.

As I struggled with seasons without income, social isolation, and rejection by the church, Jesus' prayer in the garden of Gethsemane became the ending of my daily petitions. I knew what I had to do. God never released me from my charge just as God allowed His only begotten son to go to the cross. Such had to be daunting even in the face of one who was fully human and fully divine. How much more distressing was it for a mere mortal like me?

Fortunately, I was not the first nor shall I be the last to share in Jesus' sufferings. The great cloud of witnesses kept me going. Identification with the sum of His existence is what gives believers the right to share his abundant life. We cannot cherry-pick mountaintop experiences at the exclusion of desertion, destitution, and the cross. With every downturn, I had to believe that I would rise victoriously just as our Heavenly Father raised Jesus from the dead. Despair and quitting were never options, although I gave them their fair share of consideration.

Satan has tried to break me in every way possible. Spiritual oppression began with my struggles within the organized church and manifest later through dreams deferred, social interactions (or lack thereof), health crises, and episodes of financial crises. There were times when I asked, "God, are you up there gambling with my life like Job's?" Being the contrarian I am, I pressed onward to see what the Evil One was trying to obstruct.

The church was trying to keep me from fulfilling my calling because it is bad for business. Ironically, I came to that realization not in a church, but on the couch of a Jewish psychiatrist. Corruption has become the accepted norm. It goes by another name, but the game is the same. Sexual exploitation, embezzlement, false teaching, and social control have been features of organized religion from the beginning. When members recognize them, the church gets on the defensive and runs them away.

Victims and those unwilling to go along with the lie are marginalized, ostracized, and vilified. That is why so many go along to get along while the body suffers. I was astounded to read about a pastor just two blocks from my childhood home who was convicted of raping a teenage parishioner. Her family continued to attend the church and forced her to be quiet. After she came of age and developed the courage to press charges, they left. The pastor and a deacon were convicted and imprisoned. What was the family getting from that congregation that was worth sacrificing that child's innocence?

A few years ago, I attended the funeral of a childhood friend's father at my home church—Ward Memorial AME. We not only attended Sunday School together, but also grew up in the same neighborhood, and went to the same schools. We were tight, but went our separate ways as life directed. This was not the church that was the scene of the crime. I left this one to join the latter. It was staid and traditional, but I was safe there. On the only occasion of harassment I can remember, a married man fifteen years my senior made persistent overtures toward me. Another friend's father, who was an officer of the church, nipped it in the bud. The man never bothered me again.

We had a series of pastors throughout my two decades at Ward. They were all credentialed, upstanding men. Their sermons were well-crafted and edifying. Growing up in Washington, DC in general exposed me to some of the best preaching a little Black girl could handle. The standard was high as the Nation's Capital has always had the highest concentration of educated professionals.

The same was true with preachers. During that era, it was the rule rather than the exception that preachers were trained formally in their field. Not only were they seminary graduates, a significant portion had earned doctoral degrees. I am not talking about the garden variety of vanity degrees produced by diploma mills. They had real PhDs or the equivalent which qualified them to teach in academia.

Female ministers were also common back then, at least in African Methodism. Never did the challenges they endured in the 70s and 80s cross my mind back then. Many denominations do not believe God calls women to ministry to this day, never mind significant biblical evidence to the contrary. The women in ministry in my orbit served capably and with dignity. One in particular presided over my friend's father's service. My heart leaped with delight when I saw her in the pulpit. Our paths had not crossed in almost two decades. I had seen her at a distance at conferences and other denominational activities, but we had no direct encounters.

I always feel at home when I return to Ward. The services still follow the same pattern. Familiar songs, some of which I have never heard elsewhere—are still sung. Dedicated pillars of the church continue to hold its affairs together. Ladies who I thought were old back in the day are still standing with flair. And they show me love, graciously overlooking the mischief of my youth.

The end of the service could not come fast enough. They still believe in old school processionals and recessionals. As the choir and clergy marched down the aisle with a slow cadence, I anticipated the opportunity to greet the minister. The exact words I would share had not come to me yet, but if I only got a hug it would be all right.

Being petite has its advantages. I was able to maneuver through the crowd and down the stairs to the pastor's study with ease like a skilled running back. Once inside, my face lit up as I reminded her of who I was and told her how observing her gave me strength during my pursuit of ordained ministry. She had no idea, but received my testimony enthusiastically as she prepared to depart for the interment. I gave her the sanitized version so as not to kill the mood.

She inquired where I was ministering to which I responded "wherever I am." She inevitably encouraged me, as all former church members do, to return to my roots. I uttered reflexively "it's not good for my mental health." She squeezed my hands with a knowing gaze and tears welling in her eyes. "Baby, I know" she said without any further urging. We shared an extended hug and went our separate ways. That deepened my respect for her and affirmed my commitment to remain emancipated.

Now I am no longer tormented about what could have been for me in ministry. Regardless of my lack of membership or standing in an institution, I am still called by God to preach the gospel. The church did not give that to me and the church cannot take it away. I got tired of offering drawn-out explanations of why I was not engaged in what most people perceive as ministry.

My thoughts would lose all coherence each time someone asked, "Are you ordained?" or "Where's your church?" This was out of character for one who prides herself on being driven and self-controlled. My accounts began to form a mountain of excuses that added up to no good reason why I could not execute on the charge placed upon me by God. The malicious efforts of one man and the institution enabling him could not impede the intentions of the divine. So here I am.

One of the greatest blessings throughout my twenty-five-year struggle has been my friends and family disregarding my lack of status in the organization of the church. They invite me to interpret Scripture with authority, offer blessings at special events, provide pastoral counseling, minister bedside, eulogize loved ones, and officiate weddings. Only the last am I not authorized to perform. More than a few have encouraged me to become a Justice of the Peace. I just might since the state is more receptive to my ministry than the church.

My friends call me "Reverend" knowing full well that I do not possess a certificate of ordination. They do not care. I am esteemed as such by them, nonetheless. I had the pleasure of serving as Chaplain of the Washington, DC Alumnae Chapter of Delta Sigma Theta Sorority, Inc. It was like shepherding over 500 women as I opened meetings with devotions, ministered to the sick, intervened in interpersonal disputes, and coordinated our final rites for deceased members. One of life's richest ironies is that even my agnostic friends and those of other faiths acknowledge the call on my life and wax theologically with me. A Muslim friend invited me to fast and pray with him during Ramadan one year knowing my struggle. We did not proselytize each other, but engaged in our respective acts of devotion privately with accountability. I awakened at five o'clock each morning during the designated period to have breakfast before sunrise and prayed seven times throughout the day. It was empowering.

A good friend's dad came to me as he deliberated pursuing a second career in ministry. I was astounded as he was a Civil Rights activist, former high-ranking government official, and member of a denomination not terribly receptive to women in leadership. He certainly knew no shortage of prominent and established members of the clergy. Nevertheless, he sought my counsel and continues to show me a level of respect that I have not received in my own communities of faith. He went on to pastor a New England church and commuted there weekly from DC for over a decade.

My next-door neighbor is an elderly widower. When he re-entered the dating scene following the passing of his wife, he came to me frequently for advice. One girlfriend in particular refused to allow him to spend the night at her home because she lived next door to a pastor. He told her that he likewise lived next-door to a spiritual leader and she did not seem to have a problem disrespecting ME. He has no idea how that blessed my heart.

For these reasons, I have not been able to abandon my life's purpose even when I tried. God knows I have tried. I receive calls at all hours with notifications of life events, burdens I cannot shoulder, and confidences I wish I never heard. God has also directed multitudes to me over the years who have newly discerned their calls to ministry. Seems like I have a congregation numbering almost a thousand, but without any formal title, organization, or compensation. Guess this is just another form of friends with benefits.

A United Methodist church official once told me I needed to stop performing activities reserved for clergy like serving communion and presiding over funerals. I told her the church needs to catch up with what God has authorized already or I would have to leave it behind. I do not recall any scriptural stipulations restricting who could do so. Did John the Baptist complete a qualifying process or simply do what the Lord commanded him? Jesus did not seem so concerned about his cousin's credentials before allowing him to perform the most spectacular baptism in history.

I subsequently left that church after it refused to see me as God does. Chucked the deuces and kept it moving after a long unrequited love affair. Whenever I find myself among members of one of my former churches, they feign ignorance at their offense with the detachment of the most dangerous sociopath. I do not hold it against them lest I get bitter.

What I do hold against them is their insincerity of acknowledging my gifts and graces while trying to place me in a spiritual straightjacket. That's exactly what it feels like to clip my wings in the space consecrated for the assembly of the people of the resurrection. I Thessalonians 5:19 says *do not quench the spirit.* That is exactly what Christendom requires for me to be a member. "Go about your life and forget the most defining, purposeful, and powerful aspect of it" they imply.

James Baldwin said he left the pulpit so he could preach the Gospel. The same holds true for the brand of ministry to which God has called me. What peace I have from not institutionalizing my faith. It remains intact and the guiding force of my life. My ethics, devotional life, and community-orientation have actually heightened during this period. The future is not mine to predict. I cannot say whether or not I will return to the roll of a defined congregation. In the meantime, I will continue to pursue the abundant life Jesus promised while discipling the world one soul at a time.

> *However, I consider my life worth nothing to me; my only aim is to finish the race and complete the task the Lord Jesus has given me—the task of testifying to the good news of God's grace.*

ACKNOWLEDGEMENTS

This book is dedicated to the One who knit me together, called me, saved me, and watched over my life to ensure its trials did not consume. The Lord had purpose for me long before I could even comprehend. Glory be to God for the means of inspiration, preparation, and provision to complete this project.

None of my accomplishments would have been possible without my parents who, of course, procreated me. Not only that, they loved, nurtured, and encouraged me lavishly. My mother's voracious reading habit made me the book worm I am. My father's intellectual banter prepared me for serious inquiry of ideas. Had they been born in another time and place, they would be in high places. Thomas and Hilda Brown taught me a lot about grace as I had to call home frequently when confronted with the reality of the lack of institutional support of my theological studies and vocation. Without hesitation, they met my financial shortfalls and they do not even go to church. Their sacrifices throughout my entire life have been nothing short of sacramental and I hope to return the favor in due season.

Next, my family, friends—real and virtual, teachers, and perfect strangers who have listened to me rant and moan patiently through the years. They allowed my development to unfold without forcing or forsaking me. God spoke prophetically through many who have no idea how their words edified and propelled me along my way. To all who read earlier manuscripts and improved the quality of the prose, I am deeply indebted. I am also deeply grateful for Robin Sullivan who coached me to bringing this project to fruition in her "Write to Publish" workshops.

One lifelong friend in particular became the catalyst for me casting off restraint. Dexter Poston read the earliest manuscripts and told me nobody wanted to read boring, intellectual, self-indulgent musings. He implored me during many marathon phone conversations to tell all, unleash my fire, and write in my own voice. This would have been a wholly different book without his candid feedback.

I would not have been able to maintain my sanity if not for my soulmate separated by 150 years, Søren Kierkegaard. Studying his works revealed that I am neither the first nor the last believer to struggle with the contradictions present when humanity and divinity interface. His books were life-affirming when few around me were willing to admit how crazy the church is.

Last but not least, I must express the deepest gratitude to my canine children. The late, great, Pomeranian, Trixie Lee, endured the tumult of the storm with me. She came into my life as I departed for seminary and endured 16 years of coming into my own as I worked out my salvation with fear and trembling. Ever the lady, she exuded grace and unconditional love as a reminder of God's continuous presence. Then came Phoebe Tyler, a ferocious Chihuahua rescue with absolutely no chill. She entered my life as I struggled to complete this project. Her take no prisoners style reminds me how much some things are worth fighting for. My calling and the integrity of the church are certainly among them.

NOTES

[1] James Baldwin, "Open Letter to the Born Again." <u>Baldwin Collected Essays</u>. New York: Penguin Random House Inc. (1998), p. 784.

[2] Biondi, Martha. <u>The Black Revolution on Campus</u>. Berkeley, CA: University of California Press (2012), p. 20.

[3] Duhigg, Charles. <u>The Power of Habit: Why We Do What We Do in Life and Business</u>. Canada: Doubleday (2012), p. 25.

[4] Ibid, p. 26.

[5] St. Augustine. <u>Confessions</u>. New York: Penguin Books (1961), p.21.

[6] Lincoln, C. Eric, Lawrence H. Mamiya. <u>The Black Church and the African American Experience.</u> Durham, NC: Duke University Press (1990), p. 54.

[7] Letter, George Washington to Martha Washington, June 18, 1775. Washington, DC: Tudor Place Foundation.

[8] Hunter, Rodney J. <u>Dictionary of Pastoral Care and Counseling</u>. Nashville: Abingdon Press (1990).

[9] Sack, David, M.D. (2017, June 22). "Emotional Trauma: An Often Overlooked Root of Addiction." <u>https://blogs.psychcentral.com/addiction-recovery/2012/03/emotional-trauma-addiction/</u>

[10] DePrince AP, Freyd JJ. "The Harm of Trauma: Pathological fear, shattered assumptions, or betrayal?" in J. Kauffman (ed.). <u>Loss of the Assumptive World: a theory of traumatic loss</u>. New York: Brunner-Routledge (2002), p. 71–82.

[11] Reyes, Gilbert, Jon D. Elhai, and Julian D. Ford (ed.). The Encyclopedia of Psychological Trauma. Hoboken, New Jersey: John Wiley & Sons, Inc. (2008), p. 76.

[12] Herman, Judith, M.D. Trauma and Recovery: The Aftermath of Violence—from Domestic Abuse to Political Terror. New York: Basic Books (1997), p. 33.

[13] C.J. Buys and K.L. Larsen. "Human Sympathy Groups," Psychology Reports (1979), vol 45, p. 547-553.

[14] Sartre, Jean-Paul. (1992). Being and Nothingness: The Principal Text of Modern Existentialism. New York: Washington Square Press, p. 98.

[15] Herman, p. 69.

[16] Rippetoe, Mark. Strong Enough?: Thoughts of 30 Years of Barbell Training. Wichita Falls, TX: The Aasgaard Company (2007), p. 197-198.

[17] Eugene Peterson. The Message: The Bible in Contemporary Language. Colorado Springs, CO: Navpress (2002).

[18] Rippetoe, p. 198

[19] Gibran, Kahlil. The Prophet. New York: Alfred A Knopt (1923), p. 35.

[20] Woodson, Carter G. The Miseducation of the Negro. Trenton, NJ: Africa World Press (1990), p. 61.

[21] The Onion. Vol 53, Issue 12, 3/30/17.

[22] Powell, Walter W. and Paul J. DiMaggio. The New Institutionalism in Organizational Analysis. Chicago: University of Chicago Press (1991), p. 63.

[23] McLaren, Brian. Patheos. "Seminary Is Not the Problem—the Church Is." November 1, 2011.

[24] Gonzalez, Justo L. The Story of Christianity: The Early Church to the Dawn of the Reformation. San Francisco: Harper Collins, (1984), p. 121.

[25] Chesler, Phyllis. Woman's Inhumanity to Woman. New York: Nation Books (2001), Front End Paper.

26 Jung, Carl. The Undiscovered Self: The Dilemma of the Individual in Modern Society. New York: New American Library (2006), p. 85.

27 Alter, Alexandra. Ta-Nehisi Coates Wins National Book Award, New York Times, 11/18/2015, p. A20.

28 Festinger, Leon. (1962). "Cognitive Dissonance." Scientific American, 207(4):93–107.

29 Rippon, K. A Collection of Hymns, How Firm A Foundation. (1787).

30 Lowrie, Walter. A Short Life of Kierkegaard. Princeton, NJ: Princeton University Press (1970), p. 194.

31 St. John of the Cross. John of the Cross: Selected Writings. New York: Paulist Press. (1987), p. 169.

32 Chambers, Oswald. My Utmost for His Highest. Uhrichville, OH: BarbourPublishing, Inc. (1963), November 22.

33 Jung, p. 39.

34 Ibid.

35 Rosenhan, D.L. et. al. (1973 January 19). "On being sane in insane places." Science, 179, 250-258.

36 Peck, M. Scott. People of The Lie: The Hope for Healing Human Evil. New York: Touchstone (1998), p 251.

37 Postmes, T., & Spears, R. (1998). "Deindividuation and antinormative behavior: A meta-analysis." Psychological Bulletin, 123, p. 238.

38 Moore, Thomas. Dark Nights of The Soul: A Guide to Finding Your Way Through Life's Ordeals. New York: Gotham Books (2004), p. 108.

39 Gudry, Robert H. "The New Jerusalem: People as a Place, Not a Place for a People." Novum Testamentum. XXIX, 3 (1987), p. 256.

40 Housden, Roger. Keeping the Faith Without a Religion. Boulder, CO: Sounds True (2014), p. 14.

INDEX OF BIBILICAL REFRENCES

ABOUT THE AUTHOR

DIONNE YVETTE BROWN is a minister of the gospel who has been duly anointed by God, but refused ordination by the institutional church. She has been driven by education, excellence, and ethics all her life. Those qualities did not serve her well in the church. Subsequent barriers to professional ministry have not deterred her from exercising her calling. Her writings and service are an extension of her defiant commitment to who and whose she is. Dionne earned a Bachelor of Arts from the University of Maryland, a Master of Public Policy from Duke University, and a Master of Divinity from the Candler School of Theology at Emory University.

www.dionnebrown.com